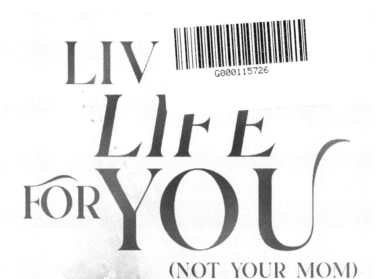

LIV LIFE FOR YOU

(NOT YOUR MOM)

EMILY S. JACOBS

Live Your Life for You, Not Your Mom

Copyright © 2022 by Live Your Life Press

Cover Design by Dee Dee Book Covers

ISBNs:
979-8-9874610-0-6
979-8-9874610-1-3

LCCN: 2022923745

Disclaimer: While this book is about mental health and wellness, it should not be used as a substitute for seeking treatment and personalized advice from a practicing clinician or professional credentialed in the mental health field.

Published by:

Live Your Life Press

DEDICATION

In memory of my mother Mary Cloutier Schmitt 1946-2020.

*To all of the daughters, in hopes that you don't feel alone,
especially mine, Elaina and Allison.*

PROLOGUE

My mother died in 2020, after a beautiful year of reconciling differences, learning forgiveness, and living in gratitude. But that was after nearly three decades of heartache between us.

For years, I shared stories about the experiences and life lessons I learned from my mother-daughter relationship, and when I did, I felt a little nudge. I had been told by friends, my massage therapist, my hairdresser, complete strangers, etc. "You should write a book about it." I laughed and thought, *who would want to read that?* My entire life, I whispered to myself, "I am not a writer." Yet, when I reflect back, I've been writing my entire life. I have yearly diaries and countless journal entries reflecting my entire life story. I've also written many research articles in my graduate schooling and even a hundred-page published doctorate thesis. *Was I trying to prove something to myself here?*

That nudge turned into a dull stab from time to time. *Should I write a book? Nah, that's not me. I am not an author.* Maybe I will just write down a few notes, as I would in my journal. But, I continued to hear, "Other women could benefit from your stories and not feel so isolated." I started believing them, however, I knew that I couldn't dare write this book while my mother was still living. She would have never understood why it was so crucial to get my message out to other women and to my own daughters. My vulnerability and honesty made my mother uncomfortable, and it would have caused even more chaos between us.

However, it still took me many years (seven to be exact) to finally accept the fact that the words of this book needed to come out of my brain and onto paper. Not to mention that I wouldn't even consider writing this until my mother passed. *How can I paint my mom in this light to the world? Am I tarnishing her legacy by sharing my pain so publicly? If I couldn't do it while she's alive, what makes me think it's the right thing to do it now, without her blessing?* HELLO, GUILT. Every time I started, I struggled with these questions.

Between 2020-2022, that dull stab turned into a razor-sharp jab that needed immediate attention. It was time to take action. It was time to write the book. It was time to provide support for women with difficult mother daughter relationships and let them know they are not alone. It was time to create support through a healing environment, through healing words and community.

I want to make it clear: this book is not about bashing my mom, but learning from her, growing with her, and deciding how my life story would be told through my writing. This book is for anyone who can relate to the conflicts that arise in the parent-child relationship. It's for the daughters (and sons) out there who are trying to understand, resolve, and determine what they hold on to and what they need to let go of to live a joyous and fulfilled life. It's for my own daughters, so they can know that, no matter what, I am trying to break that cycle for a better relationship with them.

Every word, every lesson, every section, I checked in with myself. *What was my intention? Why am I even writing this?* And, still in the back of my head, *what would she think?* Michael Singer, in his book "Untethered Soul," talks about death being the greatest teacher. He states, "Why wait until everything is taken from you before you learn to dig down deep inside yourself to reach your highest potential?" He drives the point home reflecting that death gives meaning to life.

This undoubtedly resonates with me and with her death. And here is the crazy thing, I know deep down in my heart that she is okay with this. She finds ways of telling me through flowers blooming, birds landing near my window, or a butterfly zipping by, which calms my heart. I have not felt any anxiety about writing my story, nor any doubt in my mind of how this book can serve others. Because at the heart of writing this book is my own healing journey.

I believe deep down she knows that, too. So as a side note – thank you, mom, for all of these lessons you've taught me and the growth that I accepted.

The ultimate purpose of this book is to honor the growth of our relationship and the lessons I learned to break the viscous mother daughter relationship cycle. This is a book of stories that taught me very important lessons that I can pass on to my own daughters. My hope is that you walk away with an increased awareness of the choices you can make to create the beautiful life you are meant to live (despite what your mother would think).

CONTENTS

INTRODUCTION. 1
My Mom's Story
My Story
My Daughters' Story

LESSON 1: You Are Loved and You Are Enough. 9
Judgments
Perfectionism
People Pleasing

LESSON 2: Guilt. 27
Guilt Tripping
Mom Guilt
Work Guilt

LESSON 3: Recognizing Toxicity. 43
Toxic Relationships
Toxic Work
Toxic Self

LESSON 4: Blame and Responsibility. 57
Living in Blame
Taking Responsibility

LESSON 5: You Have Control. 67
Act in Control
When Control is Lost
What You Can Control
Self-Control

LESSON 6: Choices and Boundaries. 77
Where Our Choices Come From
Setting Boundaries

LESSON 7: Shine Your Sparkling Light. 89
    Vulnerability
    Share Your Gifts
    Joy and Play
    Taking Care of Yourself

LESSON 8: Take Action. 103
    Forward Thinking
    Goals and Wins

LESSON 9: Change Your Perspective. 113
    Time
    Money
    Self-Doubt

LESSON 10: Acceptance, Forgiveness, and Gratitude. 127
    Acceptance
    Forgiveness
    Gratitude

CONCLUSION: Live Your Life For You, Not Your Mom.. . . .135

EPILOGUE. 139

REFERENCES. 147

ACKNOWLEDGEMENTS. 149

ABOUT THE AUTHOR. 159

INTRODUCTION

Mother-daughter relationships can be synergistically amazing or a downright struggle. Or for some, a mix of both. I love my mother, and my intention behind sharing my stories is to illustrate the lessons I learned from our 41-year relationship. Each lesson reflects my deeply rooted triggers and I want to use my stories as a vessel to provide a new level of awareness and much-needed hope to mothers and daughters, especially my own.

Throughout the book, you will notice a series of questions to reflect upon to dive deeper into your behaviors, actions, and choices. I suggest writing down your answers either in a journal or in the blank pages you will find at the back of this book to take notes. You can choose to read one lesson per week, take your time in reflection, and let it simmer. Or you can choose to read the entire book straight through and go back to take notes. Physically writing down your thoughts and answers is a powerful way to reflect, process, and visualize growth through your writing.

Embedded in each lesson will be my formula for healing and creating your life for you (not your mom):

1. Pause + Reflect
2. Consider Your Choices
3. Act in Alignment

My intention is for you to discover your strengths and develop tools to live a life that you love without resentment. The more you engage with this book, the more open your heart will become with small changes in your awareness and the hope I know you'll find within. I invite you to override your own judgment about what may come up as you read and experience these stories and lessons with an open heart.

This journey is for those ready to heal relationships, live more in your heart space, and move forward. Are you ready to reclaim your life and vitality? Let's begin with a little background story of my mother-daughter relationship...

MY MOM'S STORY

My mother was the oldest of nine children and basically named my grandmother's "right hand". From what I can tell, it seemed as though they expected her to help care for her eight brothers and sisters because, "That's just what I had to do," she would say in a very proud voice. She even took a pause during college to assist in caring for her family before returning. She eventually went back to become a registered nurse where she met my father, who was an internal medicine doctor. They were married for 43 years.

Family was everything to my mother. Taking care of their needs came before her own, and this was normal to her. Anything other than sacrificing herself would be considered selfish. One of her favorite mottos was, "You do what needs to be done." God forbid I complained or wanted to do anything for myself. Well, "That's just selfish." This was the mindset of the home I was raised in.

"Mom, why don't you ever do anything nice for yourself?" I asked one day. "You could go out to lunch with friends, get a manicure, go to the gym, take care of yourself, *anything*." She looked at me as if I had three eyes.

"Why would I want to do that?"

My mother went above and beyond to always be available in case anyone needed her. She was the first to volunteer to help and was always involved in every aspect of our lives. She was dependable and reliable, and we could always count on her to be there for us. Although many times this was a positive, in other ways, it could come off as very intrusive and controlling because it seemed to come with a price. For example, if I didn't take her advice, the theatrical movie of frustration followed: clenched jaw, baring teeth, slamming a door, heavy sigh, restlessness, and personal jabs.

It was equivalent to a sacrificial obsession. She needed to be needed in some way, scratch that, in *EVERY* way. Like she had to be the "go to" for *everything* and would get so hurt if we didn't ask her for advice or assistance.

It would throw her into a debilitating type of anger when I wouldn't ask her for help with something she knew a lot about. But here's the thing, she believed she knew everything, was right about everything, and that her way was the best way. Could this be because she was expected to know a lot at a young age to keep up with the demands needed in her family when she was a young girl?

Her father was a war vet who seemed to have trouble controlling his anger and tended to numb any amount of conflict with alcohol and cigarettes. So, I assume that my mother was subconsciously trying to keep the peace and not be disruptive in any way. *Was she scared to upset him?* Anytime that anyone talked about him in a negative light, she defended and protected him. "I love my father and he loved me," was her way of avoiding any deeper reflection on the subject. Could this have contributed to her hiding her emotions, bottling them up, and then exploding when the volcano erupted later in her life?

Also, it almost seemed as though she withheld teaching us some basics – firstly, because she could always do it better and faster herself, and secondly, because we would probably just do it wrong anyway (or ruin "her" laundry machine). The biggest problem was that when I did ask for help, guidance, or advice, she never really heard me or had the patience to teach me. Eventually, whatever I was doing or thought to do on my own would be so overly criticized and picked apart, it made me feel stupid and incompetent for even asking her. It was not uncommon for my mother to use guilt tripping or manipulating jabs when things weren't going her way to try to control the situation to what she wanted.

Even her very last words to us were snide when she didn't get her way on Christmas eve. Little did we all know that she would be hospitalized that evening and never return to us.

I want to add that her characteristics weren't all negative. My mom had a heart of gold but struggled with showing it in positive ways. She would compliment me, tell me she's proud of me, and show love, but only in the ways she knew how. It made total sense to me later in life, but as a child was very hard to understand. In fact,

3

I believed her heart was in the right place, and that she honestly struggled more within herself.

Over the years, this taught me that although my mother was a passionate, undeniably strong woman, she lacked a valuable piece of this "getting through life" puzzle. Her stubbornness to never admit fault or weakness, inability to be vulnerable and show softer emotions, and comparing judgmental attitudes led to a life of disappointment, high expectations, and lack of joy. Her rigidity towards self-improvement only made it more challenging to understand her own children, especially her only daughter.

MY STORY

In my younger childhood years, I can honestly attest to having the *best* mother. She was playful, vibrant, adventurous, caring, and affectionate... Honestly, I couldn't have asked for or needed anything different. She was the bomb mom! Okay, I never said that back then, but it sounded cute now. My favorite memories with her involved snuggling on the couch watching movies, her picking me up from half day kindergarten for time alone before my older brother got home, arts and crafts at the kitchen table, making cookies together, road trips, swimming in the pool all summer long, and simply just playing together.

I grew up as the middle child and only girl between two brothers. I was known as the peacemaker in the family (along with my father). Empathy really could have been my middle name. I always saw both sides to the story and looked at the big picture. However, for most of my childhood and early adult years, I grew up feeling very insecure, full of self-doubt, people pleasing, unable or afraid to say no and set boundaries, not recognizing that I had choices, and altogether inferior and small. This was a very lonely feeling, especially if you think that your situation was unique, as I did. Many of these emotions became embedded into my mindset and felt connected to the relationship I had with my mother.

About the same time I experienced adolescence, my mother went through menopause. Or so I thought, but of course, we never talked about that. During this time, everything started changing. This was the first pivotal point in my life where our relationship started deteriorating. I didn't understand what was going on and I couldn't figure out why. Was it the side by side hormonal changes occurring between both of us? Was it the unfamiliar transformations we were experiencing but too ashamed to talk about? All I remember was from this moment on, things were never the same. My relationship with my mother was an uphill battle with swords and daggers, exhaustion and defeat, and no real time for compassion and understanding.

Deborah Tannen, in her book "You're Wearing That?", explains the intricate dynamic of the mother-daughter relationship. She says, "From a daughter's point of view, the person you want to think you're perfect is the one most likely to see your faults - and tell you about them." She then says, "From a mother's point of view - any advice or suggestion you offer implies criticism."

As a young child in my school days, I can't tell you the number of times I would spend a ridiculous amount of time getting ready for school to make sure everything was perfect before I left the bathroom mirror, only to hear my mom say, "You're wearing that?" Or, "How come you didn't curl your hair today?" Or, "Looks like you're breaking out again, did you really scrub your face last night?" Every day came a new criticism or comment about how I looked. I cringed coming down the stairs every morning. To start your day with criticism over a simple "good morning" was just too much to ask for in our home.

I absorbed these comments as truth because they came from my mom, yet my body knew they felt bad and didn't belong to me. Cue the years of depression, anxiety, self-doubt, and perfectionism. You see, many times, I would just give in to make her happy because it wasn't worth the blowout fight – which usually came, anyway. I would also put so much energy into insecure thoughts. *If only I was this or if only I was more that, that would certainly make her happy.* This mindset wore me down over and over again. I felt like a trapped little caterpillar suffocating in its tiny airtight cocoon, never to see the light of day, or blossom into a beautiful butterfly.

In my adult years, I became determined to find a way to change my story, in one way, shape, or form! Enough was enough. This wasn't me, and I didn't have to live like this anymore. My first mistake was that I thought I could change my mom. I wasted so much time trying to change (fix) her. In fact, after almost every

5

major blow-out fight, my entire family would spend countless hours debriefing about all the frustrations surrounding what went wrong, what we could have done differently, and basically how to survive the next one. This went on for decades.

I made the decision to seek counseling because I just believed something wasn't right here and I was ready to choose a different path. I constantly wondered why she wasn't happy and at the same time, why I couldn't just accept her the way she was. I'll admit, I wanted her to be different. At this time in my life, I wanted a different mom.

In the midst of an argument in my 20s, she said, in a jabbing condescending tone, "I hope you have a daughter like you someday." At that moment, I snapped and said, "Yeah, me too, because I'm awesome." This is when my voice really started coming out, after years of feeling shut down by speaking up and even made fun of in school for telling "dumb" stories. I fought back this time because I finally wanted to break this cycle. I realized I no longer wanted to allow her unresolved past issues to bleed into my life.

I want to note that my parents inspired me to go into healthcare, as we all noticed that I had a natural gift of caring for and nurturing others. However, after twenty years as a professional registered nurse, holding multiple positions in the hospital setting (critical care nurse, nursing school educator, clinical nurse specialist, and corporate leadership director with a doctorate degree), I decided to choose an alternative path as a Integrative Healthcare Consultant and Nurse Wellness Coach. *This didn't surprise me!* Through individual and group coaching experiences, I now hold space for others to feel heard through deep listening without judgment, discover strengths, get unstuck, set healthy boundaries, and find joy in their life. After over 1,000 hours of coaching in my first year, I learned that I was not alone. And, that many people experienced similar feelings in their relationships with their own mothers.

MY DAUGHTERS' STORY

So, now, at the age of 43, I have two young daughters of my own and I am constantly working to ensure my relationship with my mother does not become my daughters' story, too. After years of working on myself to improve my ability to set boundaries, forgiveness, and acceptance and getting my mind to a much healthier place, I felt free. Comparable to a huge weight lifted. However, the older my daughters get, the more I experience what I call the "ugly versions" of myself as a mother and the ugly versions of my own mother shining through.

I thought I would never yell at them the way she yelled at me. I thought I would never manipulate or guilt trip them. I thought I would never do anything to hurt their feelings. *Check. Check. And, check.* I didn't understand. *Why would I show up this way for my own daughters?* My girls are now five and two years old, so yes, I am in the "thick" of it (or so I've been told). However, I didn't realize I may not have worked through all of my issues before having children of my own, and that realization can be paralyzing and debilitating. I say this because my triggers continue to knock at my door and it takes consistent effort to work through them in a healthy way.

Our first child is a fiery, passionate, emotional rocket ship full of life and energy. In fact, when I tell her birth story, I basically say that she shot out like a cannon, fast and furious, and on her own terms. By the time our oldest daughter was one year old, she had lived in three different homes (two states) and experienced three different daycares. To say she is resilient is an understatement. When she puts her mind to something, she is downright determined until completion, a characteristic she gets from both my husband and me.

Our youngest daughter was born six weeks before the 2020 pandemic. She is the bright light after the storm, the angel to comfort us and bring us pure joy. She is a nurturing caregiver at heart and pays attention to detail. In fact, in the two weeks between my mother's passing and my daughter's birth, I felt an immense spiritual awakening. It was as though the two ladies were connecting in the spiritual world together and their main mission was to take care of me. Seriously, I still feel that to this day. I know in my heart they connected.

Both of our daughters are everything we could hope to raise them to be and yet, I continue to question where I may be messing up and bringing unnecessary conflict and stress into their lives. So, I am choosing to let you in on what I am currently working on. I continue to meet them where they are in life and not where I always want them to be. This process of letting go of control is the biggest and most essential challenge I must face to have a healthy relationship with my girls. It's as if my own daughters are trying to teach me that I have more work to do and continue the journey of healing and self-improvement. Is it really true that our children are our greatest teachers? Time to start paying more attention.

LESSON 1

YOU ARE LOVED AND YOU ARE ENOUGH

Let's jump right in with the self-reflection formula. Think back to a time where you put extreme pressure on yourself and set such high expectations that you crucified yourself when they were not reached. (Or, achieved to your high standards.) I'm not talking about goals and dreaming big, I am talking about the daily anxieties, fears, and comparisons, in addition to working so hard to make others happy. I want you to spend a moment of reflection on a time when you were a kid and started thinking you weren't good enough. When your mindset shifted toward people pleasing, perfectionism, and proving yourself.

Pause + Reflect:

- When did others' opinions hold more weight than your own?
- When did you stop seeing the value of standing up for yourself?
- When did you decide that being hard on yourself was an effective method?

🦋 Can you recognize now the cost of what this may have done to your soul?

In a book titled "Parenting From the Inside Out," authors Daniel Siegel and Mary Hartzell describe how we become shaped by our experiences and unresolved issues. "Experiences that were profoundly overwhelming and may involve a deep sense of helplessness, despair, loss, terror, and perhaps betrayal are often at the root of unresolved conditions." This explains why it is so easy to repeat behaviors and patterns that we so desperately want to change. The triggering effect of the slightest negative memory can turn our best intentions into intolerable experiences for ourselves and our children. Siegel and Hartzell go on to say that, "When (our children's) lives provoke the intolerable emotion in us, our inability to be aware of it consciously and to make sense of it in our own lives leaves us at risk of being unable to tolerate it in our children." After reading this book, I became very curious as to what unresolved issues I had from my past encounters with my mom.

To start, I did not really feel emotionally safe at home. I felt judged, embarrassed, and did not live up to my mother's expectations. The disapproving look in her eye or sharp jabbing comments would completely crush my spirit. I would think to myself, *if I am not good enough for my mother, how could I be good enough for anything or anyone*? Brené Brown, in her book "Braving the Wilderness," discussed how emotions can make people uncomfortable, so many just shove it down further. She says if pain is denied and ignored, it turns into fear and hate. Even though it took an expert research professor to reveal to the world that vulnerability is not considered a weakness but more of strength and courage, it solidified and validated my theory.

As an adult, I realized there was a disconnect, and it had to be linked to something in my mother's past where she was unable to recognize, resolve, and grow from. These are the moments that I realized it's not her fault she was reactive, controlling, and judgmental, but it is her fault for not working through her behaviors or considering any growth. She never seemed to consider the negative effects she had on me. I blamed her for staying that way and not taking responsibility for her actions. I spent many years trying to describe to her that I was a little different from her and that love looked different to me than what she was giving.

The feelings I had about our different perceptions of love made perfect sense after reading "The Five Love Languages" by author Gary Chapman. This is when I started realizing that people love from different perspectives and that conflict arises when people receive and experience love differently. Chapman concluded the five different love languages are: words of affirmation, quality time, receiving gifts, acts of service, and physical touch. I highly recommend taking the quiz to determine your love language and encouraging your loved ones to as well for a better understanding of what love looks like to them.

My mom gave love through acts of services and gift giving. I remember one particular day when she was doing laundry.

"I do this because I love you," she said.

"No, you do it because it needs to be done," I replied. "That is not considered love to me."

We would argue this back and forth without any resolution, trying to prove to the other person what love is. However, after reading Chapman's book, I realized that love looked different to both of us and I could now understand her better. She still had a hard time seeing love through my eyes.

Remember, she was the oldest of nine siblings, so taking care of them was considered love in her eyes, and she didn't have space to consider other ways of love. My mother was also a registered nurse, so acts of service were how she cared for everyone. Even though this all made sense, I wish she had a little more consideration for trying to meet me where I was at.

I am more of a quality time kind of person. It doesn't matter what we are doing, I just want to be with the people I love and connect with on a deeper level. When I look back on my nursing days in the hospital, this was the part I loved the most about the nursing profession – connecting with patients and getting to know their story. It's possible that I was looking for emotional connections in others because I deeply yearned for it in my own house. Quality time and connections fill my heart with joy.

I also wanted to be heard and feel that my feelings were valid, even if those feelings were different from hers. So, I turned to my father, who would listen without judgment, accept my feelings, and meet me where I was emotionally. I never felt any change in his love for me over the years, even when I disagreed with him. He would make his point but always have space for my views. It never seemed like he had a hidden agenda. *Did my mother realize this and resent me for that?* I mean, at some point, I probably blurted out, "I wish you would love me more like dad."

My mother would always compare our relationship to other mother-daughter relationships.

"You know, your best friend calls her mom every day," she'd say. "How come we don't do that?" With a condescending tone, I thought, *Let's think about that, mom. Does she critique the hell out of her and make her feel worse after their conversation?* It was difficult to hold conversations where all I heard was everything that I was doing wrong or could do better.

It always made me wonder if my mom ever noticed disconnections or contradictions in her actions, dominating words, or behaviors. She would say one thing and do another. She acted entitled. According to her, she was allowed to leave her shoes in the middle of the mudroom, but the rest of us were not. She was allowed to portray bad behavior, yell, and scream, but got mad if anyone else acted that way. It never made sense to me.

In high school, when my older brother would get a less than perfect score in a test (close to a 95% score instead of 100%) my mom would ask, "What happened? I thought you studied." When I got an A- or B+, she congratulated me on doing so well. She would remind me that, "He is just more book smart than you," and would try to convince him to help me with my homework. I never resented my brother, but definitely felt small. *Why were the standards different for him? Why didn't she expect the same from me? Was I not capable?*

My first college acceptance letter was from my second choice school, her alma mater. Although a little excited, it disappointed me that the letter hadn't come yet from my first choice college (the school my brother got accepted into). That evening, she got a celebratory dessert for me and told me how proud she was. I really believed that her heart felt proud however she never once asked how *I* felt about it. Let me tell you, it felt bittersweet eating that desert, like it was a first place loser reward. Even though this was an elite school, I set my heart on something else. A few weeks later, an acceptance letter came from my first choice of college. I was elated! Cloud nine! *I did it.* It was a tough school to get into, and I actually did it! However, the shock on her face deflated my excitement, and I realized that the celebration had already happened.

When she did give words of affirmation and praise, it was so hard to believe. I was confused anytime she told me I looked pretty because of all her previous criticizing comments circulating in my brain. Accepting compliments from others had always been a struggle for me. I would typically follow it with a minimizing and downgrading statement. For example, if someone said, "I like your shirt," I typically responded with, "Oh, this old thing? I've had it for years, got it on the sale rack." I just couldn't muster up a simple smile and, "Thank you, that is so kind of you to say."

After decades acting this way, I also had a hard time believing the compliments to be true because I really never believed them from my own mother. It was as though it was just something we "should" say, even if we don't mean it. And then, when received, it's as if I created a mini judgment in the background that I need to justify or over explain. What I've learned is this completely downplays a meaningful compliment and eliminates the opportunity for someone to make you smile. It robs them of joy!

Tannen says that "Given how close mothers and daughters are, and how likely it is that mothers will see in their daughters reflections, rejections, or refractions of their own lives, it is not surprising that they may at times feel envious if their daughters get what their mothers wanted and could not have." Some of her comments to her friends, while talking very proudly of me, felt like she was envious or even jealous. My mother was overweight and constantly critiqued by her mother. After college, I made the decision to get back into shape and get healthier (i.e., lose the "freshman 15" that I gained a few times).

I tried to encourage her to come to the gym with me, but she was too embarrassed, "I need to lose weight first," or, "I'm too fat for the gym." A few years later, I got ripped. I was in the best shape and best health of my entire life, and I felt amazing and full of vitality.

Cue the critiques: "You're a little TOO skinny now," "What are you trying to do? Don't you think enough is enough?" and my favorite, "You look better with a little more weight." Essentially, I had to be exactly perfect to be good enough in her eyes. This is when I really stopped hearing her comments. I felt amazing and no one, not even her, was going to stomp on my vibrant parade. This was when I chose to stop absorbing her comments as the truth. Especially when I started seeing her comments reflect back on her as maybe her own form of self-criticism.

To top it off, she aimed the most painful criticisms toward the dream I had of getting married and having children of my own. She never missed a beat.

"Guess who just got married?" she'd ask. "Look who's having another child; that's four grandchildren she has already." I started talking back more.

"Good for them mom, but sounds like you aren't grateful for what you have." She denied being ungrateful with a how-dare-you tone. *Well, mom, kind of hard to tell some days.* There was always something to complain about not having.

Pause + Reflect:

- Did you ever wish to be seen as okay and enough for your mother?
- Did you ever wish you felt good enough, pretty enough, smart enough and connected this to feeling loved by her?

It seemed that any and every comment became the lack of unconditional approval and acceptance of who I was becoming. I also wondered, *did my success make my mother feel worse about herself?* She would often say, "I live vicariously through you." Maybe because I was becoming more independent, spontaneous, worldly, joyful, comfortable taking risks, and stepped outside of the norm. *Could this be why she was even more critical as I got older?*

JUDGMENTS

"You're really going to wear *that*?" My mortified mother would ask after my teenage self spent (what seemed like) hours getting ready for a single day in high school. Although this was a daily occurrence, this particular memory was during spirit week at school, and the theme was a comfy cozy day. I actually loved theme days at school because she couldn't argue with me when I was following the day's "dress code." However, just because she couldn't argue, didn't mean she couldn't have an opinion, "Ugh, sweatpants are so baggy, it's not becoming on you."

And it wasn't just clothes.

"Why don't you want to curl your hair anymore? I always wanted a curly-haired child; much more fun and cute than straight hair."

With my eyes rolled so far up in my head, I wanted to fight back but instead answered, "It just takes so long to curl my hair. And I've been so tired at school, falling asleep in class, so I decided to sleep in more this morning." (Side note: looking back, I was fatigued most of my life and I honestly think it was related to being emotionally exhausted.)

"Well, I am just saying, it really looks better curled on you," as she completely dismissed my feelings or logic. These never ending critiques later turned into, "Do you really like your hair that long?" Then, "Are you going darker? Because blonde just looks better on you."

Those kinds of questions and comments were constant, and I started to expect them, even prepare for them. As I got older, I felt that I needed to explain, justify, negotiate, and even started to speak up for myself. I believe this is when I started overanalyzing, over rationalizing, and overthinking all of my choices. Cue the second guessing and self-doubt, too. These forms of self-criticism became learned and stored feelings. By the time I tried to answer her "how was your day honey" greeting, she immediately interrupted me with 21 irrelevant questions that turned into more opportunities for judgment.

At first, I would answer her additional questions and then try to get back to my story. But the more this continued, the more angry steam bursted out of my body. *Nevermind, it's not worth it.* Wishing that I never started telling her about anything, anyway. Of course, this piled on more feelings of not being heard. What I wanted was for her to ask me more about the experiences in questions without judgment or opinion. "How did you feel about that?" Or, "What happened when?" Or, "What was that like?"

15

Anytime I wanted to talk about my feelings, she would say, "I'm not a feelings person." If the conversation got heated, because I desperately needed to express these feelings, it would turn to, "You're just too sensitive." Especially when I talked about my feelings being hurt by her name calling. "That's just the way you are taking it," or, "I didn't call you stupid, I said *that* was stupid," in relation to something I did. Again, I didn't feel heard or that she would even attempt to try to understand me. She had a defense for everything.

Pause + Reflect:

- Who do you need to be enough for?
- Is it possible that you are giving this person too much energy, power, or control?
- How is that serving you?
- What is preventing you from letting go?

For many years, I strived to be good enough for my mom and make her proud so that I could feel more love. I mentioned before that I believe she really was proud of me, but it was always so hard to accept when all I heard was criticism. I, so desperately, wanted the judgments to end and I gave this effort WAY too much power. I could't let go of the conflicting messages I was receiving from her. *Why can't she just love me the way I am? Why am I letting her comments crush me? Why do I care so much?*

CONSIDER YOUR CHOICES

Judgments are only an opinion from the person judging. Think about that. Judgments come from a place of lack. So, would it be fair to say that the person themself who is judging is actually lacking in some area of their life? Could it be possible for us to view judgments in a different light? Because here is the thing, nothing anyone says or does is about you! It is about THEM! Their opinion is only that, *their* opinion, and you have the choice to make their opinion part of your story or none of your business.

Otherwise, we are living for the opinions of others instead of considering our own thoughts about ourselves. "Someone else's opinion of you is none of your business," said Rachel Hollis in her

16

book, "Girl Wash Your Face." *Could this possibly be true with a mother's opinion? Did I take her opinions as the truth over how I felt about myself? Was I letting HER determine my opinions? Why couldn't I let some of this go?*

ACT IN ALIGNMENT

When I read that quote or speak it in presentations, it always makes me wonder how strong a mother's opinion really comes across. Would it be safe to say that a mother's (or father's) opinion carries the ultimate weight on our shoulders and is the hardest to let go? Think about where their opinion is out of alignment with you. Consider that when people judge others, they are subconsciously judging themselves and living in the world of comparison. My mother lived in a state of comparison and fear of what people would think. It made me wonder if this was at the root of her backhanded compliments... I mean, criticisms. And if she was subconsciously ultimately unhappy with herself.

I realized that no matter what she said, at any given moment, I took meaning not only from the words spoken in that moment, but also the judgment I felt from the past. And maybe she was doing the same. *So, was she holding on to judgments made by her mother? Was our relationship doomed? Would I never get over this? Would any comment out of her mouth always be considered criticizing?*

PERFECTIONISM

All of those judgments led to not feeling good enough, which led to another self-criticizing learned behavior called perfectionism.

Remember the stories I told you about getting ready for high school in the morning and checking the mirror in the bathroom 100 times before coming downstairs? What I was hoping for was her stamp of approval. I always carried a lot of hope! Because, I thought, if I was perfect, she would have nothing to comment on or judge. *WRONG. Again.* My mother noticed every little imperfection.

Well, this little learned behavior turned obsessive in high school. The minute the bell rang in between classes, I would be the first one out the door, into the bathroom to check the mirror and reapply any makeup. Any amount of acne showing just about crushed me. I started noticing every tiny imperfection and was so desperate to hide it.

I would rush to my next class hoping that everything looked perfect. My friends started catching on to this insecurity with the more makeup that I applied and called me "fakeup makeup." *Why couldn't I just let it go? Why couldn't I just be okay with the normal amount of acne that a high schooler may have?* My other friends had it and they didn't seem to care, or at least it didn't absolutely crush them. I felt paralyzed and never wanted to leave the house, but yet couldn't stand living in it. I felt lost.

After years of this, I decided to try to let it go, with the encouragement of some good friends. I changed my mindset. No matter how bad it was, and it really wasn't, I was not going to miss out. I would push through and suck it up. One of the first times that I started wearing a lot less makeup, I felt free. My face felt clean and fresh, like it could finally breathe. This was until my friend's mom saw me and asked, "What happened? Are you okay? Did you just have the chickenpox?" Seriously, another mom had to stomp on my little confidence parade. *Great, back to square one again. Maybe this is just what moms do?*

Fast forward to my young daughters examining and touching every inch of my face when we are cuddling.

"Mama, do you have a boo boo on your face?" my two-year-old daughter asks with concern.

"Yeah kiddo, mama's get boo boo's, too." She then leans in to kiss my face to help make me feel better. As insecure as I was about this in the past, it doesn't hurt as much anymore when you have a loving child trying to heal you. But still, I made my way to the bathroom to cover it up.

"Look mama, your boo boo is gone, did you just wipe it away?"

Pause + Reflect

- 🦋 What do you need to reflect on who you really are?
- 🦋 What will you accept for yourself?
- 🦋 By being a perfectionist, what is this costing you in other areas of your life?

CONSIDER YOUR CHOICES

Here is my take on it now: perfectionism is a waste of time and energy. Perfect is only an adjective to describe an opinion of something or someone. Absolutely no one and everyone can be perfect at the same time. Perfect is whatever you think it is. So, consider the powerful grip perfectionism is holding on you. Trying to be perfect is your choice.

I can't talk about perfectionism without mentioning expectations. I dread the word "expectations" and yet I still cling to this one at times. Expectations seemed to exist as another one of my mother's middle names. She was a very productive woman, a non-stop, go-getter, get sh*t done, overachiever kind of lady. Her strength and weakness still nestles deeply inside my bones, too.

The weakness came through when she expected everyone else to be on her "move a million miles a minute" page all the time. Her expectations were unrealistic and when I didn't measure up to them, she chose to belittle my choices. Especially when she proceeded to tell me all the things she had already accomplished while I "wasted the day away." These are instances where I realized that perfect and productive are subjective, not objective (as it was in her eyes).

ACT IN ALIGNMENT

As a child, I was trying to be perfect for her, but it was unnatural to me. My body knew that this characteristic was out of alignment, but I wasn't aware of the different resources that could help me. Resentment kicked in when I realized I would never fulfill all of her expectations. This only led to more self-criticizing thoughts and attempts at people pleasing.

PEOPLE PLEASING

There were times it just seemed easier to try to please my mother than to take the backlash or God forbid, even think about saying no. Can you lean in to consider where people-pleasing tendencies are not serving you? And more specifically, can you consider the relationship to your mother when you reflect on these questions?

19

Pause + Reflect

- 🦋 What would she think if you failed to fulfill an expectation she set?
- 🦋 And if you said no to her requests or suggestions, would she think you weren't capable?
- 🦋 How would you be judged then?

It seems that people pleasing and expectations go hand in hand. And, don't even get me started on obligations and those nasty, guilty thoughts that start with "*I should.*" That's a bigger topic that I will cover next. Now, I am not saying that obligations are wrong, just that in some scenarios, we need to be mindful of what it costs us.

CONSIDER YOUR CHOICES

As a child, it was easier to give in and please her. Also, I didn't want to be the one blamed in my family as "starting something" with mom. The littlest thing would set her off. I even bit my tongue and wore the ugly itchy wool sweaters and tights. (Oh did I hate tights, I can barely even touch them today!) Over time, it seemed like no matter what I did, it never helped and was never enough. There would still be something wrong or something for her to get mad about. Even if I tried to speak up, I would get immediately shut down. Can you see now where the years of self-doubt and low self-esteem came from? However, the more independent I became, she felt a loss of control and felt less needed. That was very difficult because my mom needed to be needed for just about everything.

My mom also never admitted to being unhappy or sad, almost as if discussing those emotions was a waste of energy. Although I can agree with not wallowing in it, I also believe that our bodies need to experience feelings in our own way, not controlled by others (especially our parents). This is ringing so true with my daughters. When either one of them tantrum, I sometimes try to put myself in their shoes. For whatever reason, something is going wrong for them (or they're not getting their way), and this is the way their body responds.

It is 100% up to me to allow that space for myself and my daughters to complete their stress cycle from start to finish, as authors Emily and Amelia Nagoski so eloquently describe in their book, "Burnout: The Secret to Unlocking the Stress Cycle." This works out beautifully during the times I can completely keep my cool and allow this to happen. Which I will admit, is not every time. *I mean, come on, I am not perfect. There, I admit it!* I will walk away, telling her softly and in a loving tone, "I see you are having a hard time. I will be in the kitchen when you're done and want to talk." Or, if she asks me to stay and help her calm down, I try not to talk and instead just breathe with her.

When I slip up and start rationalizing during intense emotional moments, this will cause us both to get revved up even more. This is what I call adding fuel to the fire. Sometimes it seemed my mom liked this part. She was always armed and ready for more fire. *How could someone claim to be happy and then act this way or complain most of the time? Why was she choosing this for herself and for me?*

ACT IN ALIGNMENT

As I got older, I started asking my mom, "Are you happy?" She looked at me as if I was nuts, "Of course; I'm always happy." This is what she deeply believed. But I could tell that something wasn't in alignment with her. Was she subconsciously trying to protect me or was she hiding her true feelings? When I realized this huge disconnect, I realized that her belief that "everything was fine" was a way for her to do nothing to change what she was acting unhappy about.

After years spent believing it was my responsibility to make her happy, I realized that role I'd taken on just wasn't in alignment with me anymore. Firstly, because it's nearly impossible and secondly, I realized that you really can't change anyone but yourself. I admit, I expected her to be happy with me no matter what, love me no matter what, and stop worrying about all the other insignificant stuff. As a young adult, I told her this. I told her this is how I needed my mother. But when I said this to her, I could tell that she heard me but felt challenged and couldn't understand why her behaviors were so painful for me. I was a good kid and she really was a great mom (when I was a child). I told her this too, and she responded, "Yeah, I know." Cue the eye rolling again.

The more awareness I developed, the more I spoke up when I felt something compromised my values. Peer pressure did not go over very well with me. *Could it have been because I had the biggest peer pressure-er as my mother?* I truly believed deep down that if I survived our relationship, I would do okay in the world. I had a fire inside me, similar to my mother, but different.

Despite all of this, I saw the world as optimistic. The world, not always the home I lived in, but the world. However, I didn't know how to exercise it until I had more life skills and experiences. Even as a child, I spoke up or got away from situations or people that didn't align with me. I didn't have a problem saying no, even if I got made fun of. The older I got, the more I just knew what I wanted and didn't want and felt that outside my home was where I would exercise this new skill the most.

We are responsible for recognizing the stored characteristics we embody. Every time we give in to pleasing others at our expense, we lose sight of ourselves. Consider that this enablement gives permission and paves the way for others to treat us poorly.

BREAKING THE CYCLE

I spent many years in therapy learning self-help awareness strategies and equipping the tools I needed to break these cycles and heal the wounds from my mother-daughter relationship. What I did not prepare for was the triggering effects that would return when I had daughters of my own. Only five years into this motherhood role, I continue to make decisions towards deeper reflection and continued healing. I made a commitment that what I learned from my past experiences and behaviors would be lessons for myself and for any daughter, but especially mine. I know that I am not perfect and will always be learning and growing. Each day, year, and phase we experience together, brings with it an opportunity for learning.

I am here to remind you that these ingrained responses and behaviors are changeable. Consistent to the analogy of a pendulum, I actually went the complete opposite direction in my morning grooming routine. When I became an adult, I realized how much time I was wasting and sleep I was losing with the hour-long morning primp. As a nurse, looking presentable and professional was acceptable, but rarely did nurses spend hours grooming hair and makeup just to be on your feet taking care of patients 12 hours a day in scrubs.

Actually, it became a challenge to me to see how fast I could get ready in the morning, doing just the minimum (quick shower, brush my teeth, comb my hair, and put on minimal makeup). Fifteen minutes was my fastest, however 30 minutes made me feel a little more relaxed and not rushed. This learned skill came in handy when I worked in the cardiac catheterization lab at a hospital where we would be called in overnight if a patient was having a heart attack. Talk about speed shower and even more minimal grooming because someone's life was at risk and the sooner we all arrived to help, the better recovery for the patient.

I have also considered myself a recovering perfectionist. Yes, I like things the way I like them, however I have learned to let go at the same time. Okay, my husband would stop me here to correct me in saying I am *still* learning to let go of some things. I am definitely not perfect at letting go but it's a work in progress. I do still get a little intense over things that excite me and that leads to expectations and anxiety – however with a brief pause and reflection, this can be worked on, too.

My heart still wants to hold on to perfectionism – so it's a constant daily battle. Especially with the expectations I hold on the concept of time. After I had my girls, I realized that as timely as I wanted to be, there is absolutely no way to plan for what a child will do at the last minute. Especially, when emotions come to play.

"Why don't you plan for buffer time?" asks my husband when I feel rushed.

"How much time would that be?" I reply. Because an hour seemed to be enough time to encourage the kids to go potty, brush their hair, brush their teeth, get dressed, and eat breakfast, with a few minutes to play before heading out the door. My mindset still has a hard time relaxing with the morning routine. Another part of my work in progress!

Both my daughters love picking out their clothes in the morning, which was not something I was allowed to do. Yep, my mother dressed me up until middle school. It was painful. Dressing myself was freedom that I didn't have as a child. So, I let my daughters wear anything they choose, except costumes and pajamas. Unless we have determined as a family that it's pajama day. It's still a battle sometimes to get them to choose something, anything. However, their wacky styles make them feel great. I chose (you will see that word a lot in this book) to let this one go!

I still continue to try to squeeze a lot into a little time frame and then wonder why I get overwhelmed. But, I call myself ambitious. I will say that, in addition to my style of "productivity" similar to my moms, I also take more moments to pause and reflect when anxiety or overwhelm set in.

The ultimate lesson to discover is that any of these learned behaviors or tendencies, once recognized through awareness, can be redirected. And self-assessment or self-reflection brings self-awareness and increased knowledge, hence the ongoing learning and growing. We will spend time together diving deeper into learning more of what we want to let go of and more of what we want moving forward. But it starts with unlocking and redirecting our unresolved baggage.

If we are always turning to external forces, people, situations to help us feel better, we will always be disappointed. It is not anyone's job to make us feel better. We need to look at our own accountability and learned behaviors. Peel back that onion to see a little deeper each time.

Pause + Reflect

- Who are you trying to prove something to?
- Who or what is blocking you from your best self?
- Who do you answer to at the end of the day?

CONSIDER YOUR CHOICES

Now, if you didn't answer the Pause + Reflect questions this way, think about your answers as if it were YOU. You are trying to prove something to yourself. You are blocking yourself from moving forward or past something. You are answering to yourself at the end of the day. Now, are you going to fill your mind with self-doubt, pity, shoulda woulda coulda done better attitude?

This is your permission to change your story. You are who you are, and you are enough. Repeat that out loud. Give yourself permission to say, "I made a mistake, but I am learning every day." And if you are not growing or learning, you remain stuck. Hint: after awareness, discover ways to learn from situations so as to not repeat them. A lesson that keeps showing up is a lesson unlearned.

ACT IN ALIGNMENT

Can we all make a commitment today to decide "I AM ENOUGH exactly where I am right now"? Don't minimize yourself or your successes. Don't make yourself small or put yourself down to make others feel better or more comfortable. Don't do things out of desperation, especially to be liked. If you feel as though you are "trying too hard," then you are.

Let's help change the story for ourselves and our children. To help them feel safe around us. To help them know that who they are is ENOUGH. Let's make a commitment to work on ourselves through reflection and self-discovery so that our children feel secure and loved in their own skin - not in the expectations we have set for them. And please, can you quit "shoulding" yourself now?

LESSON 2

GUILT

The judgmental, people pleasing, perfectionist feelings have the potential to lead into guilt. Guilt, at its core, implies that ugly feeling of should or should not. Which again, who are we proving this for? Remember that "should" is an opinion. If this is your opinion, you want to ask yourself *why*. Because at the heart of your "why" is the root cause driving these toxic and negative feelings.

Remember when I told you how long it took me to write this book? *Welcome back, guilt. Thanks for stopping by again.* It's clear that I worked through those feelings to create what you are reading now because I kept a promise to the book's intention. So, with that (and a little smile on my face), I am putting guilt aside to continue writing.

GUILT TRIPPING

Just to clarify, there *is* a normal feeling of guilt when we do something wrong where we can learn a lesson. However, what I am going to review here is more along the lines of guilt tripping ourself and the unnecessary guilt for not being good enough with a touch of shame.

"Using guilt as a parenting strategy takes advantage of a child's desire to please," says Lori Kaufman Rees MA, MFCS, PCC, a professional clinical counselor and life coach with Kaufman Rees Resources. When my mother realized that her power and control were not working, meaning that she felt helpless, she would throw in a sprinkle of guilt to drive a desired response. Yep, you read that right. She would try to guilt trip me into thinking that I did something wrong just because it wasn't her way.

I was born and raised in southeastern Michigan. At the age of 18, I moved out of my parent's house and never returned. From the ages of 26-39, I lived out of state, in warm and sunny Arizona. To me, this was not surprising. I was a kid who couldn't wait to be independent and live on my own means, without any help from anyone. I was stubborn, like my mom, but wanted to prove to myself that no one was in control of me anymore. I felt as if I was finally free and now believe this was the start of breaking the cycle.

I bet you can imagine that my mother did not understand that decision. She tried so many different angles through guilt tripping to get me to feel bad about moving away.

"Will you live there forever?" was my favorite comment.

"I don't know, I am here now. I don't know what forever looks like today."

"That's selfish."

I lived with these constant jabs.

Even predicting the future with, "Well, many women move back home closer to family when they have children, that's just what you do." But since I didn't have children of my own yet, she would follow with the sad, droopy responses, "I guess you will just never come home." I used to fight back more, but as I got older (and wiser), I didn't want to spend my energy adding fuel to the fire, so I just tried to change the subject or find a way to get off the phone. Her strikes slowly stopped working and I knew she could feel it.

I can't say it was very pleasant when I did return home about twice a year. Each visit was filled with attempts to control every minute of my stay. She would even start making plans for me with other family members and friends, almost like the third-party messenger without my consent. She would want every detail about who I was going to see and what I was going to do and then try more guilt tripping tactics if she didn't agree.

I learned not to give her all the details. It was exhausting how she would try to modify my plans into something she desired more.

Sometimes I would just want to come home and rest, you know, a real vacation. But that was unrealistic in my mother's house. Her minute-to-minute expectations were impossible to meet, so again, I stopped trying to fight it and just looked forward to returning to my nonjudgmental, noncritical, no expectations home in Arizona.

Nearly every time she would come visit me, "It's so ugly there, so brown. How can you like this? Oh, I just don't get it. There are no trees or green like Michigan. I like Michigan so much better." I would just smile and nod, realizing there was nothing I could change about that. And, slightly agreeing with her but… pros and cons to everything, right? So, for 13 years, I lived there. I even purchased my first home, a condo looking out into the mountains over my balcony. I felt connected and could breathe easier in the life I created for myself.

Arizona is where I met my husband, who is also from the Midwest. We chose to get married in Arizona at the most magical hidden gem of a venue that looked equivalent to a page from a European fairytale book. Drumroll the comments again.

"Why, if you are both from the Midwest would you get married in Arizona?" *Sorry, but this place was freakin' awesome.*

"Most couples get married where the woman is from, I just don't get it." Seriously, I wanted to ask her where she gets her facts from or better yet, I usually always asked, "Why?" Or, "Just because you did it this way, doesn't mean it's the right way, or only way." That only resulted in stomping, huffing and puffing, and more comments under her breath relating back to selfishness.

At the age of 39, just after my first daughter was born, my husband had the idea of moving to Michigan. This decision did not come lightly for either of us, especially him. He was raised outside of Chicago, but lived in many warm states in his adult life and never wanted to move back to the Midwest.

Meanwhile, I had always hoped that I would raise my kids in Michigan, but also wasn't attached to that idea either. Most of my extended family is in the Midwest and truthfully, we were in need of help with our daughter and our new way of life. We were both concerned about what that may be like with my mom, but in the end, we decided that it was the best decision for our family. And I still feel that way today! I will take that leap of faith as a little win.

A few months after moving back to Michigan (which I always did call my home), my dad got tickets for a college football game at my alma mater and my mom agreed to watch my daughter so we could go. In the past, this was something that we loved doing together with my brothers. However, something was different about my feelings this time.

At this point, I was working full time while my daughter was with other caretakers all week. I really only got quality time with her on the weekends. So the thought of being away at a tailgate and football game for most of that Saturday made the excitement fade. So, I made the decision to drive separately, in case I wanted to come home early to be with her.

Nothing about that decision was okay with my mom.

"How could you do this?"

"That doesn't even make sense."

"Your father was really looking forward to this and that will disappoint him."

"What's the big deal, anyway?"

"You should do this for your father."

"What if something happens to him? You will regret not going to the football game."

"What if he dies and you never get this chance again?"

Yeah, this was the worst of the worst, but you see, I was much stronger now after many years reflecting on my own, in a different state, with more positive people in my life. I lowered my head in disappointment, "I can't believe you would go there, mom. I am only going to the game if I drive separately. Unless we can agree to leave the game early if I am feeling sad and missing my daughter." I caught a glimpse of her sharp glare as she stormed back inside muttering under how breath how stupid that was.

There is another layer of guilt to this story that I need to add. You may ask why I chose to leave my daughter with her. This is something that my husband was also uncomfortable with and even my counselor at the time brought it up. If I had so many challenges growing up and even into adulthood, then why would I put my one-year-old daughter in the same environment that I grew up in? Why would I expose her to this, unsupervised?

Here is where the always hopeful, generally optimistic, little girl in me wanted to believe everything would be alright. With all of my rational thinking, logic, and reasoning, I convinced my husband that she is different around babies and children. This is true. She is the most vibrant, loving, playful (like get on the ground and really play), caring human being around children.

After my mom resigned from her nursing career, she became a kindergarten aide at the nearby elementary school and then later became the "neighborhood nanny." She was without a doubt exceptional, and families loved the care she provided, which makes sense based on her past. This skill she nailed because she was in the control seat with dependents. She treated every child she taught or cared for as her own and sincerely took pride in their upbringing. She even kept in touch with many of them as they entered adulthood. She was well-loved and respected in the community for serving in this role.

With both my husband and me working out of the house five days a week, we settled that two of those days my parents would take care of our daughter and the other three days she would go to an in-home neighborhood daycare. My husband kept trying to get it down to one day a week and my counselor still questioned any days. I used the excuse that my retired dad would be there to help. We could also save money, and, of course, I still held a deep desire to see things differently.

What I have learned is that being a mother means we constantly have to continue growing because our children are continuously growing. Meaning, I am a new mom all the time. Right now, for the first time in my life, I am a new mom to a five-year-old and a two-year-old. Never before have I had two children of these ages together and this will change again in a few months. Next year, I will be a new mom to a six-year-old and a three-year-old and so forth. My job description will change with the evolving complexities of our relationship. It is my responsibility to learn to adapt, as my daughters will, too. This is where I felt the buck stopped with my own mother. My teenage years were when I noticed she really didn't adjust her role at all and that's when our disconnection started growing faster.

Sherri Gordon, in her article, "Why Using Guilt Trips is an Ineffective Parenting Strategy," says, "Guilt tripping kids can have lasting consequences like low self-esteem." *Yep, you nailed it, Sherri.* Low self-esteem felt like my middle name for many years.

If I was always second guessing my decisions, overthinking, worrying about the outcome, worrying if anyone would be mad, and striving for perfection (that never really went smoothly), it makes sense my self-esteem and confidence in myself were taking hits left and right.

This utter lack of self-confidence bled into feelings of shame. Oftentimes, I had the desire to fade into the background or believed I deserved this pain. It became difficult to trust myself and that turned into risk-taking behaviors. Over time, I had a deeper desire to do everything on my own, like *everything*. And as another way to fight back, I would reject help out of a desire to do a penance or be a martyr. Not having the validation that you are doing okay from your mom, can make it very hard to find it internally. This led to disappointment in myself for not being able to "help" myself break the cycle all those years.

MOM GUILT

Guilt is an automatic response, triggered by thoughts, emotions, or unresolved issues. However, much of our guilt comes from a lack of trust, primarily with ourself. Many of the women that I coach bring up mom guilt that started as a brand new mom and persisted as they became seasoned mothers. Many of these guilt-feeling issues stem from how they were raised and possibly from unhealed junk from their parents' past experiences and upbringing. So, here we are, new at motherhood, not trusting our gut or believing in ourselves, second guessing ourselves, and then feeling guilty for our choices. This is a recipe for disaster. *At least for me it was.*

Research shows how mom guilt starts when the baby is in utero and then intensifies throughout time. You can literally feel guilty for just about anything when you are pregnant. Here we go with "shoulding" on ourselves again. *I shouldn't have eaten that. I should drive slower. I should be more productive. I should buy all of the informative baby books and even attempt to read them, or just make my partner read them. We should finish everything on our "to do" list before the baby arrives.* Do you see how these feelings of stress, overwhelm, and guilt are circulating around our body right before a major life transition? Not to add more guilt, but the baby feels this!

Pause + Reflect

🦋 What is at the heart of mom guilt?

🦋 Is it rooted in those feelings of not being good enough?

🦋 Are you trying to prove something to yourself?

🦋 Who are you trying to measure up to?

Mom guilt is often rooted in fear. Fear that we aren't doing enough for our children. Fear that we aren't loving them enough. Fear that our mistakes are haunting us and will affect our child's life forever. Fear that we should have done something differently. This is a lot of unnecessary toxic thoughts circulating through our brain.

WORK GUILT

In my private practice, what I have learned is that guilt is different for everyone and comes in many shapes and sizes. As a healthcare professional, I've learned that we are prone to caring for others, even at our own expense. I remember those days well. As a nurse in the cardiothoracic intensive care unit (ICU), I would be the first provider recovering a patient from open heart surgery. The patient came back to the ICU on a ventilator (which is a machine that breathes for them) and multiple intravenous medication drips to keep their heart rate and blood pressure titrated at a specific range. This range was something that I controlled by increasing or decreasing the vasoactive medication at the right time and waiting for the desired response. *A little intense? Yes, I can see that now.*

So bathroom breaks were a luxury unless you could find another nurse to cover. It was not uncommon to hear a nurse say that they never got a chance to go to the bathroom on an eight – or 12-hour shift. From the outside looking in, it may be easy to say, "Just walk away and go to the bathroom." However, when someone's life is on the line, it's not that easy. My tasks and responsibilities were heightened due to staffing shortage issues, and created another form of guilt I carried.

Nowadays, I am hearing things like:

"I can't take a day off because then we would be even shorter staffed."

"My team needs me."

"I keep getting calls from my manager to pick up extra shifts because they need help."

So, we rationalize guilt and think that being logical will help. *I guess I could use the money. It feels good to help out; I don't want my team to suffer.* We can rationalize workplace guilt when we find it easier to care for others than ourselves. However, this leads to burnout.

Here, we again can see the guilt, obligation, people pleasing characteristics that enhance burnout, overwhelm, exhaustion, and stress. I had a manager tell me, "that was a fail," when I didn't roll out a massive new project over a scheduled, approved vacation time. Even though the committee changed the date during a meeting while I was away and moved up the project. This mindset trains you to think that it's more productive, valuable, helpful, and that you "should" go into work even when you are sick and even on your day off.

One of my clients is a medical doctor who was home sick with a fever and vomiting. Guess what? Yep, she felt guilty and even lazy for being home and had a hard time resting and taking care of herself. She thought she should be more productive and felt bad for her colleagues who had to work even more hours while she was out. So, she agreed to try and do some tele-health work to assist.

"What treatment would you advise your patient if they experienced the same illness?" I asked.

"Lots of fluids, rest, recover, antibiotics, and take it easy," she responded.

"So, it's advised for them but considered lazy for you?" With a deliberate I-told-you-so tone, I then asked her, "Would you consider taking out your prescription pad and writing yourself the same treatment, post it on your mirror, and when you feel lazy, take a look at what a doctor recommends?" She smiled and realized how badly guilt was sucking out her remaining recovering energy.

Another client stated that she hadn't taken a vacation day in two years!

"Why?" I asked her, simply.

She stated, "I wasn't allowed to." *WHAT?!* My mouth fell open.

"What do you mean?" Her boss told her that it wasn't possible with the staffing needs. And if she wanted to take a day off, the manager needed four to six months in advance, to consider if it even gets approved.

"What if you get sick tomorrow?" She agreed with me.

"Right? I don't know." *Wait. What?* The veins were popping out of my arms at this point. She even told me that she would pray she would get sick just to get a day off. That just seemed so incredibly sad and backward to me in the healthcare system. *Were the leaders playing on providers' feelings of caring for others and using their guilt against them?* I'm picturing the manipulative, "Well you got into this profession to help people, right?" *I can just hear it now.* What was happening here? How are we missing the boat on this one? Okay, that's my rant for now. Because that would need another entire book!

I used healthcare professionals as a reference, however I realize this could be any caretaking job and really any profession. But we can't blame work for everything. Especially when we choose it because we don't value the short amount of time off we have to recover and take care of ourselves. So, guess what usually comes next? Complaining, blaming, and the victim mentality when you allowed the feelings of guilt and "should" overpower your own wellbeing.

Pause + Reflect

- Do you dedicate all your time and energy to giving to others?
- Do you feel guilty about taking time for yourself?
- Do you have guilt for not missing your child and enjoying work?
- Do you feel guilty for not feeling guilty?

That last one is odd to say, but really happens to some women, especially when returning to work. Thoughts surrounding, *why don't I feel bad about this? Aren't I supposed to feel more guilty for returning to work? Can I love my job and at the same time love my children and being a mother? Is this even possible?*

Hot Topic Alert: returning to work after maternity leave or taking time off with kids brings in another high level of emotion. Lauren Smith Brody, in her book, "The Fifth Trimester: The

Working Mom's Guide to Style, Sanity, & Success After Baby," works to empower the mother transitioning back into the workforce in their new identity. Mothers returning to work after any amount of time off will come back with a different set of values, priorities, feelings, and emotions. There is a discomfort during this transitional time. If you are in this situation now, here are some reflection questions:

Pause + Reflect

- ❧ How do you be transparent with your needs without sounding needy? Hint: give and take or propose a trial. Your needs and wants will change as your baby does.
- ❧ How do you feel about the caretaker of your child while you are at work? Do you have any feelings of resentment?
- ❧ How do you feel about your non-parent colleagues? Do you act "mom-perior" around them?

Remember, this is all temporary! You are returning to work a different person with different values and priorities. Try not to work harder, this is a marathon, not a sprint. Take note of self-criticism and have grace with your sleep-deprived self. Remember your worth and values and celebrate small wins.

CONSIDER YOUR CHOICES

Start with making a list of where you experience the most guilt. What fears lie behind these thoughts? Write your thoughts on paper and read them back. How does it feel to see those words and what do you wish you could change? What can you control and what emotional energy feels as though it is drowning you down?

The whole key is starting with awareness. Once you are aware that you are feeling that way again, you can choose to pause and reflect, and then make a different choice. Check in with yourself. *Is this really how I want to be feeling right now? Where is this coming from? What is it trying to tell me about myself?*

Another exercise to practice is bringing to light our negative self-talk and how this really doesn't serve any of us. Here are some examples of negative self-talk:

My child deserves better.

I am such a terrible mom.
I am a failure.
This is the way it will always be.
I wasn't cut out for this.
I can't do anything right.

And on and on until we are wallowing in self-pity and victim mentality. So, when you hear this negative talk enter your brain, BOOM you have awareness. Next, pause and reflect. *What is really true here? What am I making up because I am sad, angry, tired, etc.?* Then, replace it with something more true, positive, or encouraging.

Here are some examples to reflect on this with a more positive approach:

I wonder why I reacted this way.
I made a mistake.
I am human and learning.
I didn't like that choice.
Next time I will do better.
One day at a time. One moment at a time.

Are you catching my drift? Bad moments do not make you a bad person. You can re-direct the moment anytime. You have the power to change your thoughts. This concept was mind-blowing and life changing for me. I am not my thoughts. Repeat that back to yourself. *I am not my thoughts.*

ACT IN ALIGNMENT

Here are some positive affirmations that you can reflect on in moments of weakness. Consider which one of these statements best fits for what you're feeling:

I am not a bad person/mom for_____.
I am not a failure because I didn't _____.
I am not a monster for _____.
I am not my mistakes!!!

PSA for parents: your kids don't need you to be perfect. In fact, they are not even expecting that from you. They just want you to love them, no matter what. They want to feel love, a sense of belonging, and really just be safe. Did you hear me? *You don't have to be perfect!* Because, even if your parents didn't admit to it, guess what, they aren't either (and deep down they know that, too). Here is where switching mindsets from negative self-talk to positive self-talk can be very helpful in your daily experiences.

Another question to reflect on is: What would your child say if you opened up about how you were feeling? Like, how you were *really* feeling on the inside? With young kids, a sample could be something like, "Sometimes, mommies get frustrated and yell. It's not your fault, mommy's heart is feeling hot and angry." And then follow in a softer tone with, "Do you ever feel that way?" Or if your children are older, really connect with them and let them in. Trust me, this will connect you both on a deeper level. And, in some beautiful way, your child may become your best teacher, supporter, and encourager.

What example are we setting for our kids if we live a life full of exhaustion, anxiety, guilt, complaints, and negativity? Are we teaching them that this is what life is all about? Are we teaching them to accept or even tolerate this behavior from their friends, bosses, parents, colleagues? Or do we want better for them? Don't get me wrong, I am not trying to make you feel guilty by any means. I am simply bringing your attention to the bigger picture of what really matters, and what's at the heart of a joyful life. Our children determine what normalcy is based on how they are brought up in this world. However, they will also make their own decisions moving forward about what is normal for them. If we don't want them to mirror our lives, then maybe we need to look in the mirror.

BREAKING THE CYCLE

Speaking of mirrors, can you look at one and say out loud to yourself, "I am worthy of love and belonging"? Brené Brown is an academic research professor, author, and podcast host known for her research on vulnerability, shame, and leadership. Seriously, if you haven't heard of this woman, check her out. You will not be disappointed. "No matter what gets done and how much is left undone, I am enough. It's going to bed at night thinking, Yes, I am imperfect and vulnerable and sometimes afraid, but that doesn't change the truth that I am also brave and worthy of love and belonging." I can't possibly write a book about these lessons without a few pointers from one of the experts.

Connect with other like-minded women, whether in your community, support groups, secret tribe, anything. Not to just bitch and vent (yes, a little is okay) but then make a pact to help each other through mom guilt instead of drowning in it. Having other people to reflect with and ask for accountability can really help, especially when we experience barriers that want to pull us back into our old traps. It's very easy to do. There will always be barriers because our ego wants to bring us back to that negative mindset. That's what it is most used to. That's the cycle we are all trying to break.

Pause + Reflect

- How will you face guilt when it comes knocking back at my door?
- What will you say?

CONSIDER YOUR CHOICES

Try to recognize guilt's sneaky little face pop in and out of your life. When we stop trying to shove it back down and actually examine it on the surface, it starts to lose its power. No, seriously, try it. When you start dissecting it apart (even for just a split second in the moment), notice what happens. By drawing a little attention to guilt, it's not controlling you anymore. You start taking the driver's seat. *Hi, I see you, but I really don't want you here right now. Can you come back later?* I know, I know, sounds silly, but I encourage you to try it next time you are aware.

ACT IN ALIGNMENT

Then the next step in breaking the cycle after you pause and reflect is to consider replacing guilt with something more positive. Have you ever considered the power of "I am" statements? I am statements strengthen your brain and fill it with more confident loving feelings. This is another method to re-train our brain into more positive self-talk. Let's try it together now:

I am worth it; I am strong; I forgive myself. I am learning. I am _____.

Take a few minutes to jot down a few of your own I am statements. Then, take a few deep breaths, read them out loud and try to really feel them to be true, even if it's hard.

39

What happened in your body?
What feelings came up when you wrote these down?
How hard or easy was this exercise?
Sit with that for a minute. Could you come up with any more?

Once you have written down some I am statements, next post these around your home or set reminders on your phone or really anywhere you need a reminder of who you are. I even had a client use a dry erase marker to write it in her bathroom mirror, where she would look at it every morning. What if the first thing we saw every morning was something that made us feel good about ourselves? Sounds like a pretty good start to the day!

This next exercise is essential (in my opinion) to help get out of these self-doubting, guilty moments. Take about five to ten minutes to jot down some pivotal moments in your life where you can look back feeling proud, renewed, rejuvenated, and accomplished. These are what I refer to as Wonder Woman Moments. Feel free to come up with your own title. You know, those moments that you thought, *holy crap, that seemed so challenging at the time, but it isn't anymore*. It felt as if the world was ending, or you were so uncomfortable making a change and yet you overcame it, accomplished it, or moved past something negative, toxic, difficult.

Remember writing these moments down now is a way to reflect on them later and visualize or even re-live them for a moment. So light a candle or diffuse essential oils, play some inspiring music, or just be silent for a few moments and think back on your life. There are super power moments that got you to where you are today.

What did you come up with? I bet none of them had anything to do with guilt, self-doubt, or people pleasing. No! Because these were moments of confidence, empowerment, achievement, just outright *HELL YEAH - You go girl* moments. Now, go back to these moments and jot down your age, just as a timeline point. You can even put them in order.

Pause + Reflect

How does it feel to reflect on these?

- How does anything you are experiencing now, or any area you are stuck in, compare to these moments?
- Are you able to feel any relief in what you are going through now?
- Are you able to see the big picture, any clarity, any light in how you may overcome the next thing?

You've overcome things in your past, perhaps multiple times. Now, I am not saying any of this is comfortable, but it is doable. And it helps pull you out of that negative self-talk and guilt-driven obligatory choices. So, here is your permission to pull out this Wonder Woman list *anytime*. Because you may need a little refresher of how far you've come in this lifetime. Glance at it anytime you are doubting yourself or what you are capable of. Remember the Wonder Woman strong human that you are. And, remember this point that I really want to drive home: MOM GUILT IS A BIG FAT HAIRY UGLY LIAR. So, what do you say? Time to take that trash out?

LESSON 3

RECOGNIZING TOXICITY

Learning to recognize the toxic patterns of negative energy are essential in breaking cycles and moving forward. This could be anything from working in a toxic environment, being in a toxic relationship, or your own internal toxic energies. If we choose to remain stuck living in these environments or allow that environment to exist within ourselves, how can we ever move past them? And diving a little deeper, what are we gaining by holding onto these toxicities? Hint: we must be gaining something if we aren't willing to let it go.

So, here comes that word "awareness" again. Once we become aware that a toxicity is present, take it one step further and pay attention to how your body feels in these situations. There may be some clear signals indicating what your physical body is trying to tell your mind. Let's take a moment and reflect on more questions.

Pause + Reflect

- Pick a situation, environment, or person that you feel a lot of toxic energy around and ask:
- What is serving you? What is not serving you?
- How does it feel in this environment, around this person, within yourself?

43

🦋 By holding on, how is this blocking you from moving forward?

🦋 How do you want to feel and what are the feelings on the other side of this toxicity?

🦋 If this toxicity didn't exist, what would it free up for you? What would that space feel like?

This is just an exercise to get us to bring awareness to our own emotions and reasoning with toxicity. Being honest with ourselves is part of that initial awareness. I realize that this section may not be easy, so have some grace with yourself as you read through it.

TOXIC RELATIONSHIPS

Let's take a look at the people we surround ourselves the most with: our family, friends, partners, co-workers, managers, and community.

Have you ever experienced a negative or toxic family member? Someone you just can't stand to be around; maybe they are constantly complaining. Everything always seems wrong or off, and you just don't feel any sort of joy being near them. You sense a negative energy in the tone of their voice or even physical tension in your body when you are near them. And, to top it all off, after a period of time with this person, you have experienced your body starting to absorb this person's energy, thus leading to a more irritable you. Energy works through osmosis; it is absorbed into everything it touches. It's as though your body can't resist adapting to this energy because it's easier to join in than fight back.

There were many interactions that I felt toxic energy sensations around my mother. Whether it be in conversations or just being in the same room, everything just felt tense and challenging. As a teenager and young adult, I chose to accept that this was the way it was and thought it would always be this way. I remember a time when we were just having a "normal" conversation in our family room, or so I thought. Don't get me wrong, a normal conversation consisted of 200 questions with side comments and lots of opinions, but still, normal for us. I remember the expected sprinkle of criticism and small doses of disapproval intertwined. What started as our usual type of conversation heated up (as it sometimes would do).

The intensity of this particular conversation grew and became unmanageable for me to handle. It must have hit every insecure nerve and trigger that I ever experienced all at once. My body shut down. Completely and utterly shut off. I felt outside myself. I couldn't speak. I felt like I couldn't breathe, cry, *nothing*. The room started appearing dark. I curled up in a ball on the floor, knees to chest, shaking like a frightened child. Time stopped. *What was happening? Why was I going into a protective mode?* These were just words, words that I was used to hearing for many years.

My mother appeared confused yet calm, like it's not a big deal that her daughter is having some sort of panic/anxiety attack. *Did she subconsciously realize that she had finally broken me down completely?* A few seconds later (it felt like hours), I was able to take a few deep breaths, uncurl my legs, and stand up. At that point, I felt as though I freed myself, freed myself from her chains, but I couldn't make sense of it at the time. My legs felt a little numb, but I still managed to walk towards the door saying, "I can't be here right now." I never knew how my mom interpreted that day. I never asked her because I knew that it really didn't matter to me what she thought happened. I needed to start letting this piece of her go.

Later, I realized, over and over again, that it was my decision to keep putting myself in scenarios where I could get hurt by her. I kept hoping for a different outcome. I kept wishing things were the way they used to be when I was a young child and felt that initial unconditional love. It's as if I really couldn't accept that we weren't ever going back to that type of nurturing relationship.

And then something else happened. I started having gratitude, which shocked even me. I started thanking her for showing me how strong I really need to be in this world to survive. Because if I could survive her, I would probably be just fine! Yes, this is the full(ish) circle that I am experiencing now. I have come to peace with our relationship and have gratitude for what we both went through in the process. I can only imagine that this wasn't easy for her, but I won't really know to what extent as she wasn't an expressive "feelings" type of person. And believe me, I tried to dig deeper into her brain.

Around that time of my life, I also started thinking about all the things I did for my family out of obligation and how I felt doing them. Which ones was I going to accept and which ones were sucking the light out of my soulful heart. Which obligations would I keep and hold on to with hopes it would make things better? Hopes it would make *her* happier. Hopes it would make things more positive and easier for my family. So many times exhausting myself doing things out of obligation only made me feel worse about the amount of effort I put in. *For what?* Sometimes, absolutely nothing. NADA. Like it was all a waste. Then, the worst feeling arose... being mad at myself for thinking it would actually be different each time.

Now, I am not saying *not* to do things for your family out of obligation, but check in with yourself first.

Pause + Reflect

- ⟿ How are you really handling your assumed and assigned obligations?
- ⟿ Is this in true alignment with you?
- ⟿ Could you take on this obligation without negative feelings?
- ⟿ How do you want to really feel?

CONSIDER YOUR CHOICES

If you choose to continue with said obligation, then own that decision all on your own without expectations. Decide what energy you will bring. Also, decide how you will protect that energy if things go sideways. I started always planning my "out" just like I did that day, curled up in a ball. If you live in the same house with a toxic family member, consider ways to protect your beautiful energy.

PARTNERS (AND FRIENDS)

I have been coaching many people who talk about toxicity with their chosen partner or chosen friendships. They feel stuck in the fear of what's on the other side of not being in that toxic relationship. This is a shorter section because I have realized how deeply sensitive this topic can be, especially with a partner. I am only trying to bring awareness. Which, if you are in this type of relationship, you have already noticed the disconnect in what you are feeling between what you are saying and your actions around it by choosing to stay. Enabling unacceptable behavior tells that person that you are okay with it and it gives that person permission to continue without consequences. Just consider the disconnections and think about how you want to feel. Consider how you really want to feel in a partnership and in a relationship. Most women I've talked to want to feel valued, appreciated, loved, and heard (at least most of the time). So, if these are not the predominant feelings at the core of your relationship in the big picture, consider some reflection.

Pause + Reflect

- What is serving you? What is not serving you?
- What are the strengths of your relationship? What do you agree on?
- Generally speaking, how do you feel when you're around this person?
- What are you holding on to that feels driven by fear or obligation?
- How is this fear blocking you from what you really want or how you really want to feel?

Listen to your body. It will give you the answer.

CONSIDER YOUR CHOICES

Motivational speaker Jim Rohn said, "You are the average of the five people you spend the most time with. The people you spend the most time with shape who you are."

Start with writing down the people you spend the most time with and narrow this down to five. Jot down some feelings you get when you are around these people and what kind of energy they bring.

What do you like or dislike most about them?

Pause for a moment. What do you think about these results?

Take a few minutes to write down what you think these results mean to you.

Overall, do they make you happy or angry, or disappointed, or have a desire to change?

Let's take this one a step forward. Next, write down the people in your life who bring more positive energy when you are around them. Like, even when they are having a bad day, you still sense good energy coming from their body or voice. These people light you up and you feel a beautiful electric spark near them. Maybe this is the protector person who brings you calmness, comfort, safety, and peace. Or this is your head cheerleader who encourages the crap out of you and won't let you fail. Or the coach who pushes you away from your comfort zone when you feel stuck and holds you accountable to create your life on your terms.

Keep in mind, these people do not have to be very close to you anymore. This is just a reflection on those who stand out or even made a difference in your life. After you jot down a few names, pause and reflect again. Is there anyone on this list you could be closer to, spend more time with, and bring more exposure to your life? Think about this possibility. And don't forget that even though you don't live close to each other, modern technology has benefits here, so anything is possible if you want to get closer to people you enjoy.

ACT IN ALIGNMENT

Do you want to know the secret to creating your tribe? Start with shining a light on these individuals who truly fuel your fire in a more positive light. These people lift you up, believe in you, and believe in your big dreams. You have already determined that surrounding yourself with them for any amount of time has already benefitted you in some way. Start by reaching out and thanking them for what they have done for you and see what happens. *Don't* chase a friendship or force it to happen. Just set the stage and see what transpires.

Consider that other people are on their own journey, and it may not involve you right now. It's okay, now that you are more aware of these kinds of people, the ones you need will show up more. Free up space in your heart to let go of toxic people, which will make room for those who build you up.

Many of us have unrealistic expectations that one person (a partner, best friend, mother, father, sibling, etc.) should have all of these qualities all the time. If you have one person that does, that's really great, a unicorn, a gem! However, it would be unfair for us to put that kind of pressure on anyone else and could honestly set them up for failure. I realized that I had expected my mother to be everything I needed, because why not? She's my mother. Once this awareness started sinking in, I started thinking, *would I want this kind of pressure on myself? How could one ever measure up to that?*

Time to look in the mirror and start to recognize the reality that there are billions of people on this planet. We can find a few that can share in feeding our soul so we aren't dependent on just one. And, how about what you expect from yourself? How you show up is how you are perceived and what kind of people you attract. Your true vibe attracts your ultimate tribe.

TOXIC WORK

Working in the healthcare field for over 20 years, I came to expect that employers should care for the employees who take care of their patients. *Just sayin', it only made sense to me.* When I first started as a nurse in the hospital, back in 2001, it was a privilege and an honor to be a nurse working at a prestigious hospital. I did not take this for granted and did my very best to care for my patients.

However, it seemed that the healthcare system shifted sometime around 2010 into more of a business with corporate-driven expectations. The responsibilities and tasks became increasingly prioritized above the care for the patient. It seemed this was the start of healthcare administration trying to do more with less and the start of toxic work environments in healthcare. Less staffing, fewer resources, but more responsibility and checking the boxes for insurance companies. The pressures were high on employees, managers, and administration to produce. *Produce what? Aren't we just here to take care of people? Was this a result of the 2008 recession and loss of money?* I wondered about this often. Because shortly after, the standard, models, and workflow started shifting.

My first major toxic experience was in 2017 (during my first pregnancy) where the Chief Nursing Officer started questioning my workflow. This was after 13 years as a Clinical Nurse Specialist (CNS) and Nurse Educator, at the same hospital, running many nursing programs successfully, onboarding hundreds of nurses, evaluating the competency of experienced and new nurses, teaching dozens of classes a year, and in charge of all the education requirements for the nurses throughout five cardiac units of the hospital. Mind you, the other CNS/Educators were only responsible for one to two nursing units at this facility.

I also reported to *way* too many leaders (three managers and two directors), who all had conflicting educational ideas, desires, and "asks" but for about 10 of those years, I managed to satisfy most of their requests. That was until I proposed hiring more help.

"Emily, the only way we could justify getting another person is for you to start falling short and showing us there is a real need here," said my director. *What? No! I'm not doing that, I am not going to have that on my employee record.* And that's how they got me! I learned that in this field, the harder you worked, the more work you got.

After I returned from maternity leave, they made false accusations on my record related to a simple miscommunication. The manager took my badge and put me on administrative leave without giving me the opportunity to explain myself. I felt humiliated as they walked me out – trying not to make eye contact with anyone. I was informed that a representative from Human Resources would be contacting me.

When I finally had a chance to tell my story, I was 16 weeks post-partum and just dropped my daughter off for the first week at daycare. I was in a room with the person who wrote me up and the HR representative. I could barely even get a sentence out without either one of them interrupting with disbelieving attacking comments. I felt defeated, my chest numb and limbs heavy. Nothing I said was being heard; there was no consideration for accepting any part of my story, and I felt set up. Since I knew that I couldn't prove it, I decided not to fight the system. I walked myself out, resigned on the spot, and never returned. I could not believe a company that I dedicated my heart to would treat me this way. I felt confused and betrayed.

Towards the end of my nursing career, I was promoted to a corporate nursing leadership position in a major healthcare system. Eve Rodsky, transformational leader, change agent, and author of "Unicorn Space," shouts at us to dream big, face our fears, and find a legacy in our gifts. Rodsky inspires us to find our gifts, then find a space in the world that appreciates that gift. I believed the nursing world needed a powerful and empathetic leader that would stand up for the profession, keep the passion alive, and coach nurses towards empowerment over burnout and exhaustion. I decided to have a seat at the table. A place where we ran systems, wrote policies, and developed programs to grow the employees who take care of the patients. *Yes, this is where I was meant to be.*

Except that it was the most toxic place I had ever encountered. Apparently, I walked into a raging fire. Funny how they don't tell you that in the interview. There were reports of bullying among leaders, employees who feared speaking up after previous retaliations, and basically the complete opposite of what you would read about in the company's code of conduct. I felt physically sick. *Now what? Do I try to step up to the plate and go to war with a major corporation?*

I had two choices: stay and fight the system or politely resign from something that no longer aligns well with me. This time, I did try to fight for what was right. I couldn't sleep at night and when I did, dreaded the alarm in the morning. It was that anxiety bell ringing in my ear saying, *get back to it! What would people think if you left so soon? You failed. You can't afford to quit. It's not that bad. Don't leave your employees, they need you. Keep speaking up. Don't give up.*

Thankfully, I only spent a short time in this space before I realized, it's not worth my mental decline and that this wasn't a place to serve my beautiful gifts. After six months of contemplation, I let go of the paralyzing attachments, logical reasons to stay, and ultimate drive for a better system. I decided that I couldn't work for a company that supported, tolerated, and enabled this toxic environment. It's no wonder toxic places have a hard time retaining staff.

"Burned-out, stressed-out, and frazzled leaders foster organizations that experience high turnover, low employee engagement, steep healthcare costs, and dysfunctional teams that often work against each other," said Jim Dethmer, one of the three authors of "The 15 Commitments of Conscious Leadership: A New Paradigm for Sustainable Success." They go on to say that dullness and workaholism is a true epidemic destroying our companies and our people. And yet, we continue to see it over and over again.

The 2020 pandemic revealed an extremely unsafe workload model in healthcare. The hospital systems expected nurses to basically do everyone's job and pushed harder for them to maintain this as their "new normal" even two years later. Nurses were on the edge of the burnout cliff prior to the pandemic and are now plummeting off it with resentment and anger all circulating around not feeling valued or appreciated. In all my years, I had never seen burnout happen so quickly for new nurses who are now leaving the entire profession after two short years. "Business" at the hospital pushed through any chance of recovery for their employees and are still now expecting them to "produce" at even higher and unreasonable rates.

This is one of the main reasons that I started my own company: to work for myself and report to myself. I realized that my work environment plays a huge role in productivity, creativity, inspiration, mental health, and purpose. I took a scary leap of faith, trusted my heart, and made the decision to create a healthy work environment for myself, all on my own. I continue to fight the systems allowing these behaviors. I continue to empower others to stand up for themselves and bring awareness to the importance of recognizing these toxic detrimental effects on their health.

TOXIC SELF

This is a tough one. Check in with yourself. Really check in. What energy are you bringing forth every day? What energy do you bring to each relationship? This may vary from moment to moment, day by day, or depending on our experiences and circumstances. Either way, start developing awareness of how you show up.

When my husband and I lived in Arizona, we loved going to the local farmer's market. Shortly after my first daughter was born in 2017, we decided to stop by, running into our birth doula.

"How's it going?" she asked, knowing that it was a loaded question to a new mom. Well, I couldn't hold back.

"Not good. I am drowning, exhausted, and it's just a constant struggle every day."

"What is your energy like?" she asked. *Huh,* I thought, *MY energy.*

"What do you mean?"

"What's your energy like in your home?"

I had never really spent any effort or time reflecting on our energy, but I told her that six weeks into being a new mom, I was at my wit's end. It felt as though that question was a huge (very huge) slap in the face. *What do you mean, "how's the energy?"* I am certain I had steam coming out of my ears when I responded.

"It's horrible. We are exhausted, fighting, and I can't think straight. I feel completely lost and alone. The baby cries all the time. No one is sleeping. This is just not what I expected. Why is it so hard?" Here came the next pivotal sucker punch.

"Well, you are going to need to change that."

Are you for real, lady? You really think I can add one more thing to my plate? I almost collapsed on the sidewalk that day. *How could she say that? How could I possibly put any more energy or time, add one more thing on my "to do" list, let alone CHANGE?* I waved the white flag in defeat.

She recognized my reaction as if this was common for new moms and handed me a phone number of a woman to call, who would know just how to help me. And she did! This is the moment I started creating my "mom tribe." A group of women in motherhood who pulled me out of the dark hole and helped me to not feel so alone in my journey. Elizabeth Wood is a saint and the founder of Matrescence: 4th Trimester Planning and Support. Her mission is to empower women during their transition into motherhood through providing resources, workshops, and group support. She genuinely saved my exhausted soul.

This encounter was my first proper introduction to understanding how energy affects everything. This tired, complaining, negative mindset that I was bringing into my brand new baby's world was not okay. It was not okay for me, my husband, or really anyone around me. This was a very painful reflection on the last six weeks and how I contributed to our environment. *Yep, I saw it. Ouch.* What happened? My negative energy was pushing people away, and it's no wonder we were struggling.

It was no wonder my daughter struggled with breast feeding with her mother's arms holding her with intensity and force. It all started making sense. I didn't have the energy to get mad at myself or depressed about what was happening. But, I decided to get help, find a tribe, become aware of my energy, and start having grace with myself. We did not have an easy go at it the first time around, which was no one's fault. But we did have control over our energy. From that one day, I started breathing easier and looking for solutions instead of drowning in quicksand. This is an imperfect and constant lesson that I still carry with me today. Multiple times a day, I practice checking in with my energy, especially being a mother to very strong young daughters.

Pause + Reflect

- Check in with yourself. Are you acting stressed, irritable, or angry?
- Can you relate it to something specific (hungry, tired, overwhelmed)?
- Or is it deeper like, unresolved triggers or unhealed wounds that are knocking on your door? Or both?
- If so, where do you need to go back inside in reflection and work on these?
- Consider, are you acting negatively because something in your life feels out of my control?
- And last, how can you stop projecting this energy onto your family?

CONSIDER YOUR CHOICES

For me, I reflect on what is the key priority, big picture, and value of acting this way. And to top it all off, my five-year-old daughter calls out my energy now, too.

"Mom, can you make your face softer when you talk to me? Your eyebrows look mean." She noticed my tense lips and tone as I was trying to get out the door on time.

"Well, honey, did you hear me the first couple of times when I asked you nicely?" I firmly stated as I tried to hold back the explosive burst of volcanic anger.

So, yes, I get a little stern and direct all with the intent of *not* yelling. At the same time, reminding myself that I am still the parent here. Trust me, some of these moments take every single ounce left of my patience to take a deep breath and see the big picture. But I promise you this: when it works, it works magically and beautifully and inspires me to check in more with myself and my energy.

I have also noticed that when my energy is negative, it trickles down to the rest of my family like a contagious virus. My kids start whining more and my husband becomes more distant. The energy of the house is negative and chaotic. Now, it's not my responsibility to take care of everyone's energy, but it's just a gentle reflection of how I am showing up and how that may affect others close to me. This is growth.

ACT IN ALIGNMENT

Recognizing the energy you bring is important, especially if you are hoping for something different. Check in with yourself first. Take a deep breath. Consider changing your energy to reflect how you want to show up. All of this could take as little as one to two seconds or if time allots, spend a few deeps breaths in this space creating a positive intention. This is available to you and I give you permission to use it anytime. Now, it's time to give yourself permission to actually practice it.

BREAKING THE CYCLE

This chapter is not my favorite, and as I am writing it, my stomach turns. Recognizing toxicity is one thing, but actually taking action is a greater challenge. It's scary not knowing what's on the other side. *Cue fear of the unknown.*

I had been a part of the healthcare system for over 20 years, and I unconditionally loved being a nurse. It just kept causing me pain to see what the system was doing over and over again and not realizing how it was destroying one of the most trusted professions. It hurt and it still hurts. There are times I still yearn to do more (maybe in the next book) but it doesn't align with my values right now.

When I learned how to recognize toxicity, I started paying more attention to where it was showing up for me and how I felt around certain people or certain environments. It was and is still difficult to admit that I had a toxic relationship with my own mother. The little girl in me still wants to always paint her and our relationship in a positive light. But that's just not our story. And I am learning that we were given exactly what we needed in our relationship together.

It's hard to admit when I bring toxic energy into my life, my home, and around my children. This is where I harvest the most guilt and need the most reflection. I share these stories because I know that I am not alone, and I am hoping that some or even one of them may resonate with you and inspire you to take a look at the bigger picture. "We are not here on this earth to be working in a 'soul crushing' job," said one of my clients who felt trapped. We are not here on this earth to be robots, micromanaged, and controlled beyond our limits. Some will try, some may even succeed, but even now, in this moment, we can change our own direction. We don't have to enable this or tolerate this anymore. Whose life is this, anyway? How do we start to take responsibility for this one life we are living?

LESSON 4

BLAME AND RESPONSIBILITY

Through my years of coaching, I have noticed a common thread that links our personality characteristics to unresolved issues and experiences that we haven't learned to move on from. Many of my clients talk about the things they didn't enjoy about their past, wish never happened, or wish they could go back and change. If I'm not mistaken, I would say the majority of us wish we could go back in time and said something or done something different. *Shocker alert: we can't!* We can't change the past. No matter how hard we try. There is a lot of energy spent thinking about the past or allowing the past to continue in our lives today.

LIVING IN BLAME

Let's be honest, many of us have wanted to blame someone else for where our lives are right now or for how we feel. It would be easy for me to place blame on my mother. Trust me, I spent a ton of time in that space. Part of me felt good to have someone to blame for my negative characteristics or even negative experiences. Little voices in my head would even validate this. *She did this to me. She made me this way. I am this way because of her. It's not my fault. There is nothing I can do about it.* Yet, I continued to feel hopeless and helpless, like I would never break free from being her victim.

This was a very powerless feeling. It seemed as though every time I tried, I heard criticizing words in my head, some of which were hers and some of my own self-doubt. Those triggering words paralyzed me over and over again through most of my adult years.

My mother acted comparable to a martyr with a consistent blame-filled connotation in her undertone. "I sacrificed my life for my kids." I remember thinking, *I never asked you to do that.* As a child, I really didn't understand what this even meant. I thought you just had children because you wanted to. No one forced you into this role. Now, here's the thing: my mother was a very proud woman. She wore her motherhood roles and responsibilities like a badge of honor. However, it seemed to me that she was not happy with her sacrificial actions. She made it very clear that her children's needs came first, above any of her own needs. It was very selfless. However, I could see this wearing on her. It was especially noticeable when her physical health, emotional well-being, and spirit started declining in her early 50s.

I realize now that the "this is just what you do" phrase she always said was loaded with a background of unhealed wounds from her past. There was a tone in her voice that revealed sadness, regret, and envy when she would say that she couldn't do this or couldn't do that "because of my kids." She always made it sound as if she didn't have a choice. My mom even blamed my dad because he suggested that she didn't return to work after having children because she was needed more at home.

If you haven't figured this out already, my mom was a strong-willed woman, so I doubt she was passive or submissive when it came to making these decisions. But she made it her "blame" story for many, many years, and you could definitely feel her resentment. I always wondered, if she was that unhappy about it, why didn't she do anything to change that? *Seriously, the woman who worked to control every outcome took a back seat?* After my older brother and I were in grade school, she did look into going back to work part time. However, after my younger brother was born, those thoughts ended. She even agreed with my dad that staying home would be best, even though you could hear her resenting undertone.

After I graduated from nursing school, I started studying for the board examination to obtain my registered nursing license. I remember my mom saying how proud she was of me and that maybe she would even re-take her nursing board exam and go back to work. She undeniably loved being a nurse and was truly elated when I chose this profession. However, she regretted letting her license expire (which consisted of paying the renewal fees and either keeping up with the educational and/or work requirements). So, I challenged her.

"Let's study and take the boards together." I saw a tiny smile and spark light up in her face. Like, *huh, that's not such a bad idea.*

"I *was* a damn good nurse. Everyone loved me," she commented in a prideful voice. Then, proceeded with many stories around this belief just to drive the point across. She talked about other colleagues who are still working and the pure joy she had working in the hospital. It was a beautiful conversation filled with exciting energy, laughter, and hope.

"Let's see what you got, mom!" I said, ready to share something positive with her.

Well, that didn't last long. Only a day or two after this conversation, her excitement came to a screeching halt. She started down the path of self-doubt, insecurities, excuses, fears... you get the picture. Her logic and reason for not doing it became her reality. The discomfort of actually pursuing this career again in her 50s was a little too daunting for my mother. I definitely don't blame her, but still wanted to challenge her, too. Mainly, so she would stop complaining about it.

As a mother myself, I know this can be hard. After my first daughter was born and I walked out of that toxic job, I wondered what I was supposed to do next. I wondered what my purpose was. *As if being a mother wasn't enough.* I had always associated my career with who I was and now I'm "just a mom." I felt lost and alone again. The tired exhausted new mom felt that there must be more than this. *Insert guilt feelings again.*

I knew I was meant to make a difference in this world and just couldn't feel that where I was. That, and my whole life just got flipped upside down and had to re-discover myself. So, I made a choice to stay stuck in comfortable jobs knowing that I was meant for more but making excuses that "I had to do this for the family" with a blaming undertone. At the same time, feeling similar to the default person for managing everything in the house and with our daughter. Mind you, I have a very supportive husband, but it was a difficult adjustment. Why were our own fears and doubts preventing us from dreaming bigger and holding us back?

Gary Hendricks, author of "The Big Leap," talks about how to recognize our "upper limit." This is a term he uses to describe that once we attain a higher level of joy, happiness, or success we then often create drama in other areas of our lives to prevent us from going any further and to bring us back down. Have you ever noticed that you can be so happy and excited in one moment and then you destroy it? Almost as if your mind was telling you that it was too good to be true and it's time to bring it back down.

He also talks about studying your worry habits because worry is an addiction. Worry has nothing to do with what is actually happening right now and it's a way to avoid feeling the flow of positive energy. We subconsciously block ourselves from joy every time we start to worry. He talks about learning how to spot your upper limit which can be imbedded in criticism, blame, deflecting, avoiding compliments, arguments, and breaching integrity.

In "Untethered Soul," Singer takes it one step future when he discusses how everything has two extremes, and the challenge is finding the middle way (the center). "If you pull a pendulum out one way, it will swing back just that far the other way." The true secret is not entertaining or getting lost in the extremes and finding balance in the center. The medical world calls this "maintaining homeostasis." One could view the mother-daughter relationship swinging from a pendulum in an upper limit cycle of destruction. The harder one pulls in one direction, the harder the other pulls in the opposite despite her.

Pause + Reflect

- What do you think this is caused by?
- Did your mother allude to blaming your success on her lack of success?
- Do you think this is caused by envy? Or jealousy?
- Is this caused by having a fear of not taking that chance and now she has regrets?

CONSIDER YOUR CHOICES

Blame is thinking, *because of them or that situation, I am now unable to create a life that I hoped for, that I love.* Think about how much power is in that statement. It's almost as if you decided that a particular person or situation is the owner of your life, and you are going to live in the victim mentality. Let me guess, if you feel this way, it does not feel like you are in control of your life. Like someone put you here and you are stuck in this dark hole.

But here is the thing: blame is an absolute waste of energy. Total and complete waste of time. And in my story, over two decades worth of time wasted. That's a lot of freakin' time, people! And trust me when I say, I am still working on this! The triggers don't go away, but I've learned to work with them and work towards those triggers not crushing me every time they rear their ugly little head.

I spent years in therapy because I didn't realize that I was actually *gaining* something from this so-called blame/victim mentality. If I continued to live in the space where I blamed my mom for causing my depression and anxiety, it was just easier to live with that story. It made sense why. And I guess that worked for me. It was her fault, and I wasn't going to let that go. The emotional trauma experienced from my mother was unique (or so I thought). And, after a while, I couldn't even imagine not having it. This was our story.

Blame had created a home in my body, and I let it stay and get comfortable. Too comfortable. Here is the clincher: I was comfortably uncomfortable in this space. What I mean by that is I got used to my discomforts as the new norm and this was the way it would always be... in a constant state of discomfort. However, I always knew that something didn't feel right and a piece of my spark and my joy were missing from this story. The act of blame that I was holding on to did nothing for me. I thought it was helping, but it became exhausting and annoying. I chose blame to be my "act" and my "story."

ACT IN ALIGNMENT

Your act can turn something that is not real (or not real anymore) into something very tangible if you let it. Your act is the story you keep telling yourself (and is your inability to break free from). These stories started at a young age and made a comfy, cozy home inside you. In fact, if you keep your "act" going, it's easy to repeat and never move past it. This then becomes *your* story and part of who you are.

Yes, this can be true if you let it, or you can change your story. Because this act will keep appearing until you show it that it no longer serves you. Let's consider this for a second: what happened, happened. What didn't happen, didn't happen. Reflect on the facts and not the story you are filling in between. Remember, it's not your fault you got here; it's your fault if you choose to stay here in this story.

In this exact moment right now, can you recognize that it's only a trigger? It's something from your past saying, "Hi, remember me?" And in that moment, you can decide if you're going to let it inside to play or choose a different response. Has any good ever come from blame? Spending energy in the mindset where others are blamed for your misfortune – it will rob you of your joy. It strips your soul of your true potential. It is 100% not your fault for whatever person or situation has harmed you in any way! However, it is your responsibility to act if you want to get out of this space. Period.

Eleanor Roosevelt said it best, "No one can make you feel inferior without your consent." Are you ready to write a new story?

TAKING RESPONSIBILITY

It is not by accident that you chose a certain relationship, job, friend, place to live, your home, school, etc. Think about your choices. Where can you start to take responsibility? Consider taking 100% responsibility for where your life is right now. This means to stop blaming others, let go of being right, and be a solution to your own life.

This starts with recognizing where you hold blame and expectations, because this usually sets us up for constant disappointment. Consider areas of your life where you expect others to take care of you, yet you are not taking care of yourself. Think about how backwards that sounds. Continuously working on breaking this cycle takes work, but it gets easier with more practice.

Pause + Reflect

- Where in your life are you not taking full responsibility?
- Where are you distracting yourself from what really matters? (I.e., look at your health and wellbeing first.)
- Where and when do you feel the most alive?
- If there were no obstacles, how do you get more of that?
- Where can you learn to forgive and let go instead of feeling stuck?

CONSIDER YOUR CHOICES

I check in with myself frequently because we all go through cycles and phases where we need a gentle reminder again. Growth is an essential piece of not staying stuck in the same repetitive cycles. Learn to be honest with yourself and take responsibility so you can make a different choice.

ACT IN ALIGNMENT

Don Miguel Ruiz, in his book, "The Four Agreements," says, "Nothing others do is because of you. What others say and do is a projection of their own reality, their own dream." Take that in and really think about that. If someone is unhappy with themselves, they usually project, in some way, onto others. Because it's easier to project than dive deeper and work on yourself. There really is no pain with projecting.

I didn't know about this concept when I was younger and it was very hard when the unconstructive criticisms came from my mother. I believe children just want to feel loved and that their parents are proud of us. However, criticism from parents can come across as mean and unintentionally hurtful. So can we just repeat this out loud? *Nothing anyone says is about you, it's about them.* You get to decide what parts you take and what parts you leave.

And please try to remember this when you feel criticized in unhealthy ways. You have the choice to absorb this internally or make the decision to leave it out of your body. I told my mother that I needed her more for support and encouragement, and then when I had children, remind me that I am a good mom, too. We worked on this for a few years before she passed, and it was unequivocally the best part of our relationship. It started with my forgiveness and letting go of how we expected each other to be and just allowed ourselves to be our own person without blame. We took responsibility for how we showed up (most of the time).

Self-reflection starts with awareness first and then assessing how you're feeling and what changes you desire to make. Where can you lean into letting go of harboring negative feelings? I know it's difficult, but what does not letting go continue to give you? Forgiveness is the start of a healthy path towards increased honesty, self-compassion, grace, patience, and love for yourself.

How, you ask?

Stop trying to one up yourself and start being proud of yourself. Stop looking further ahead for happiness and look right in front of you. We will also discuss this more a little later but, for now, here are some resources to bring more happiness and positivity into your life.

BREAKING THE CYCLE

Shawn Achor is a Harvard graduate and leading expert on success and happiness. In his book, "The Happiness Advantage," he asserts that we need to reverse the formula, "if I work harder, I will be more successful," and then I will be happier. So, believing that happiness is on the other side of success is backwards. He says, "Happiness is not the belief that we don't need to change; it is the realization that we can." Our optimism levels, our social support, and our ability to see stress as a challenge instead of a threat predict success. He discusses how we can re-train our brain in 21 days through daily gratitude, body movement, acts of kindness, and medication or prayer. Sounds like a worthwhile experiment to me.

If I have learned one thing from coaching and entrepreneurship, it would be this: being stagnant, making excuses, and blame is being comfortable (or comfortably uncomfortable, as I mentioned previously). And growth takes a little discomfort and discipline, which is not easy. There is no easy out to this one. No quick fix here. If you were trying to get stronger at the gym and even hire a trainer to help, even they aren't going to do your push-ups for you!

Here is the big question – would you rather get a little uncomfortable for an extraordinary life or remain stuck in the life you are constantly complaining about?

Start by taking responsibility. Right now, I definitely feel that it is my responsibility to break this pattern of blame and break this cycle for a better relationship with my own daughters. I had blamed my mom for causing my self-doubt, insecurities, and years of self-help therapy. *She did that to me.* But not anymore. Once I let go and broke free from the control that blame held over me, I was no longer a victim in that story anymore. It is 100% my responsibility to create the life I want starting today. So, are you with me? Are you ready to take responsibility for where your life is *right now*?

Make a commitment: from this day forward, I will _____. Or, I will not _____.

Releasing this grip with a forgiving mindset will free up space for the beautiful next chapters of your life.

LESSON 5

YOU HAVE CONTROL

What is being in control? Is it the power over others or over a situation? Is it feeling as though you have it all together? Is it keeping calm despite the chaos? And then, when you feel as if you are losing control, do you feel overwhelmed and like things are unmanageable?

ACT OF CONTROL

My mother constantly tried to *control* everyone and every situation in our family. She would then be upset if her manipulative methods were unsuccessful. This next story definitely made history in one of my top three mom stories. In fact, these next stories were the ones where I would hear, "you should write a book," when I shared them with others.

In terms of letting go, I wish my mom could have let go of the need to control me. I wish she could have let go of how she wanted me to need her instead of how I really needed her. You see, she wanted me to need her for everything, *every little thing*. Even if I learned how to do something myself, she felt hurt, "How come you didn't call me? I could have helped." Or when I decided to paint a room in my new condo, "I've done that a thousand times and could have told you how to do it the right way," with her offensive tone insinuating, "How dare you not even reach out?". Mind you, she took no account of my excitement about what I accomplished.

My mom acted especially controlling when it came to me getting married and having children. She never missed a beat in sending me little jabbing comments reminding me of all of my other friends who were getting married or about how many grandchildren her friends were having. It became a frequent tally of where everyone else was, and where I fell short. A way to rub it in a little, or make me feel bad, or even force me to speed it up.

"Just tell him you're getting married, end of story," I recall her commanding me once in a very stern, direct voice. "You're not getting any younger; what are you waiting for? What's the problem?" This was at my ripe young age of 26 with my first real boyfriend after about four years of dating. We had talked about it someday, but didn't feel rushed.

"We are fine where we are, and really happy." This just boggled her mind. The look on her face was confused.

"I don't get it. You can be happy when you're married, too," lips tense as she stormed off.

Over time, those comments got into my head. The "What's he waiting for?" and "What's the problem?" started deflating any happy little thoughts in my brain. *Maybe she's right.* I started questioning why our relationship wasn't moving forward, which created really ugly, unnecessary doubt. In the year following, we moved in together and I started pushing harder to get married, which created hesitancy on his end. These emotions grew more severe to the point of experiencing my first officially diagnosed depression and anxiety symptoms. *Where did my elation and joy go? I had been happy. Why did anything have to change? Why did I let these comments take control over me?* The self-doubt and questioning myself became so severe that I started medication and sought counseling to help with this new emotional pain.

He eventually proposed, but when it came to setting an actual wedding date, he kept postponing it (three times to be exact). And with each time, these emotions became more and more severe. *Why is this happening? Why doesn't he want to marry me? I don't get it. We were so happy.* Even my therapist suggested delaying the wedding (noting the red flags that I couldn't see). Some of my friends would even add, "It shouldn't be this hard before you are married."

Although I agreed, I felt completely defeated, alone, and lost. I remember thinking, *where did I go wrong?* Then came the "shoulding" on myself. *I shouldn't have pushed so hard. I should keep my thoughts and feelings to myself. I should stop listening to everyone else and go back to being happy again.* And then, all those "shoulds" started distracting me from dealing with the underlying issues. *I should do more around the house. I should go back to graduate school. I should just drop it for the weekend and see if he comes running back.* Of course, none of those worked. I tried and tried, which only ended in more defeat and self-doubt. Maybe he really doesn't love me that much. And then the dreaded, *maybe it's really not meant to be.*

So, yes, after a few years of this indefinite engagement. I decided to take my control back. I couldn't feel this way anymore. So, I moved out of his house, put a hold on the engagement, and just freed myself. It felt empowering. I started taking care of myself and find the missing piece of *her* again. This was not a tactic to get him to do anything or a threat anymore; I just needed space. Just being in a new environment allowed my heart to open up and it felt so good. I started realizing the disconnect between his words and actions. I realized my own disconnect between how my heart felt versus my own actions. *In what world did I ever dream of having to convince someone to marry me? NEVER!* This was not okay with me. After all of this hesitation and postponing, would I even trust him to show up on the actual wedding day?

One morning, I woke up crying. Like a big, huge, get-it-all-out cry. To this day, it was the longest cry of my life. I felt comparable to the holy spirit putting his hands around my throat and started choking the oxygen out of my body. I had a hard time breathing. When it finally stopped, I felt paralyzed just lying sinking heavy into my bed. I had completely exhausted every part of my mental and emotional and physical body, like an overcooked burnt meal just sitting there cooling off.

But then something very strange happened. It's almost as though this was an unconscious big release of all that negative self-talk, toxic energy, and struggle. I started feeling better, more empowered, and had the strength to release that *I am in control* of my life. Like, really in control. I do not have to put myself through this anymore. As hard as it was to believe, I trusted these thoughts. I repeated them over and over again. *I do not have to put myself through this anymore.* I knew, without a shadow of a doubt, that I needed to move on and that I would be okay.

At that moment, I knew I needed to break off the relationship. I just had to trust this was the right decision. I remember the exact moment that I ended the relationship. I started breathing more fully. I stood up taller and had faith that this bold decision would change my life for the better. "Sometimes choosing to walk away, even if it means breaking your own heart, can be the greatest act of self-love you have access to," said Rachel Hollis, in her book "Girl Wash Your Face."

You see, I realized that I could control my own outcome here and start changing the parts of my story that no longer served me. I stopped depending on someone else or this particular situation to determine where my future would go. I stopped feeling handcuffed by someone else's decisions. I also realized in this moment that I would be fine. I would be okay. As you can imagine, this did not happen overnight. But when it happened, it was parallel to a bolt of lightning shooting through my body. It was up to me. Up to me to determine the life that I wanted. Up to me to decide how I was going to show up and let go. Up to me to find myself again. With each day feeling lighter, I started recognizing myself again and even being proud of letting go of something I held on very tight to. It was no longer serving me.

WHEN CONTROL IS LOST

Our efforts to control others or manipulate situations can backfire and contribute to us living in the worst versions of ourselves. Think about how much energy can go into controlling something, especially if it's not working. It's exhausting. The harder the resistance, the harder you try to achieve your desired outcome.

Well, this next story occurs shortly after that first engagement. My mother, aunt, best friend, and her mother came to town and we went bridal dress shopping. Now, I did my research and pretty much knew the dress I wanted, but also wanted to have fun trying on others, too. So, I picked about five dresses and saved my favorite one until the end. I knew the moment I put the dress on; it was the one. I felt shivers down my spine and pure joy in my heart. *When you know, you know!* So, I came out of the dressing room and showed everyone. Smiles everywhere. They knew, too. Well, everyone except my mom. She was disappointed. Not because I found the dress that I loved but because we were done, and she had a hard time accepting that I decided so quickly. Maybe she was just used to years of my indecisions and self-doubt. *Well, not today.*

I didn't let her attitude get to me this time. Nothing was going to stomp on my happy parade. I can only imagine this bothered her, too. She was used to me fighting back, arguing, adding fuel to a passionate fire. I just decided, *not today, not worth it.* Especially in this moment!

So, we decided that since I picked my dress out, we would start looking for the bridesmaids' dresses, which I also narrowed down very quickly. I really let my best friend pick the ones she liked the most and just would hope the other bridesmaids would be fine with it. All I really cared about was that they were simple, elegant, and classy. By the third dress she tried on, we knew it was perfect. We both stood there in our chosen dresses, smiling, joyous, and happy about sharing this beautiful day together.

My mom had returned to us after gathering more dresses to try on only to experience more disappointment that were done.

"Don't you think you should put more thought into it? That one is just okay, it's nothing special. Here, try these ones that I picked out."

We both, very confidently and without hesitation, said, "Nope, we are all set."

She had missed out. She missed out on the moments of pure elation in her daughter's heart. All of my mom's negative energy was defeating her, and she felt it. She dramatically sat down with a loud sigh, held up the dress she picked and said, "Well, fine then. Maybe I will get skinny enough and wear this one. I like it and I don't care what you think." I remember thinking, *sure, mom, whatever you want.* We all knew she was losing it.

With extreme body tension and exaggerated movements, she rolled up the dress around her crossed arms similar to a mad child, holding it tight to her chest. The store attendant came over to check on us and asked how we were doing. I told her our decision was made and we would take these two dresses and thanked her for her help. The attendant started gathering the other dresses and then approached my mom.

"May I take that one to put back, please?"

"NO, I'm keeping it, it's mine… I'm gonna wear it. Or … or maybe cut it up and use the fabric to make purses out of it!"

What had happened here? She could have been a part of a very special moment for her daughter and instead chose to act like an absolute child because things weren't going her way. Either way, I was not playing into that today. As I checked out, still not getting that smile off my face, I told the attendant, "Thank you for putting up with all of us." And her response was classic, "Well, I have a two-year-old at home, so I'm used to this. Good luck." Light bulbs! I have a two-year-old, too, only mine was my mother. She had an utterly child-like tantrum in the middle of a bridal store when things didn't go her way. *Huh…* new awareness sinking in. Adults can have tantrums and it's best not to play into them.

WHAT YOU CAN CONTROL

Well, now that I have toddlers of my own, I guess it was good that I got a little head start learning about tantrums. What I realized with this experience was that something was triggering my mom to react this way. *Was it an unresolved issue from her past? Was it the emotions around her daughter finally getting married? Was it expectations about this day being all about her and fulfilling her needs? Was she unhappy about something in herself and projecting it on us?*

When triggers are induced and emotions are high, mindfulness and self-awareness can be a challenge. More often, we react to the situation as if it was a personal attack instead of really hearing what is being said. And, even if it really was a personal attack, we can still have control over our response.

I've noticed that when my daughters tantrum and feel their world is crashing in on them, it's related to something they can't control. *Mainly, because I am trying to control something.* At first, I would be empathetic to try to help them, fix it, negotiate, or even give in. That's when I realized they got me. They knew how to control those situations because they discovered my weakness (trying to please).

In Emily Nagoski's book "Burnout: The Secret to Unlocking the Stress Cycle," she reveals the normalcy of stress and helps the reader identify tools to complete the stress cycle. Because the alternative is to bottle it up, shove it down, and believe it will go away. Yes, for many years, that sounded about right for me and for my mother.

Instead of dealing with stress or having tools to complete the stress cycle, I did whatever I could to make it disappear. Alcohol, distraction methods, worked overtime and extra jobs, squeezed too much into a brief time span, overbooked myself... you get the picture. Never dealing with our stress builds up to become our own unhealed chronic diseases. These were big "ah-ha" moments for me.

Even though my mom was an adult, she didn't have the tools to manage her big emotions. I see that now as a lack of knowledge or support. This comes full circle when my girls start to tantrum and I fight back, it's as though I'm really fighting myself. When I try to rush them out the door or get angry for not getting ready fast enough, it's related to my lack of control over time. Again, none of this is bad, but when I push and push, and then push harder, it always backfires. It starts with awareness and then creating a new direction.

Pause + Reflect

- Do you recognize a stress response about to happen right before it actually happens?
- Where do you feel it in your body?
- What do you do to cover up stress instead of dealing with it?
- Do(es) your method(s) serve you in any way, or make you feel better?
- What could you replace with a healthier alternative?

CONSIDER YOUR CHOICES

I am continuously working on my reactions to my daughters' tantrums, whining, four million questions, and just trying not to yell at them. In the seconds before I am about to scream or yell at my kids, I notice my body getting really tense, warm, irritable, steam wanting to burst out of my ears. Every little noise starts to feel similar to nails on a chalkboard that I become a volcano about to erupt. In this moment, once I am aware it's happening, I know I have two choices. Yelling, snapping, screaming is one way which is quick, feels powerful, and feels like I am in control.

However, this leaves my body deflated because I feel as though I turned into a monster. This method is much harder to recover from and then I end up apologizing to my kids. I apologize because I know it's my fault for reacting that way.

The alternative choice would be to take a short pause, deep breath, and realize this isn't personal and ask myself, *how do I want to show up right now? How is this serving me?* In both of these responses, I have full control over my decision. I have a choice to explode, or I can approach it with a calm, direct, unemotional response. This short pause allows me to reflect on which method serves me at the moment and why I needed that response. The calmer response doesn't retain that stress in my body. It actually never really even lets it all the way in. So, the more I choose that response, the better I feel. And, yes, I still yell at my kids sometimes. I'm not perfect.

ACT IN ALIGNMENT

Consistency and continuous self-reflection lead to an increased awareness and the ability to change your natural reaction. This is where inner strength meets your unhealed wounds and works towards breaking these cycles. This is also where you can start to learn where you feel disconnected and how to act more in alignment with the best version of yourself.

SELF-CONTROL

What is not serving you, is destroying you. It's exhausting to keep complaining about the same things repeatedly without taking accountability and responsibility. If this is you, just consider how this way of life is serving you. Consider that you become a slave to whatever it is that you are complaining about.

Pause + Reflect

- Where did you lose control with feeling guilt and the need for people pleasing?
- What are you allowing in your life that doesn't serve you or align with you anymore?
- Where can you see that by allowing this (behavior, person, situation) that you are enabling it by giving more permission?
- What are you trying to control? Be really honest here.
- What are your fears about letting go?
- What is one action you can take today to move forward in better alignment with yourself?

CONSIDER YOUR CHOICES

Currently, I am learning to find the balance between guiding my daughters and letting them make their own choices. Whenever possible and appropriate, I let them make their own choices within reason. I have realized that both of our daughters want more control and exercising it in a healthy way has been helpful. They hate being told what to do – we all do. I can see and understand this now. That being said, sometimes it is necessary, especially in a dangerous situation, which is why I said "whenever possible."

Control is hard to let go of, especially as a parent. Our children go from being completely dependent to learning how and desiring to do things on their own at such a young age. I now realize how much of a challenge this was for my mom when her "dependents" started becoming more independent and having a voice. I just hoped she would grow alongside us.

ACT IN ALIGNMENT

In my adult years, I decided that instead of reacting defensively to my mother, I would use a different approach. This was in hopes of achieving a different outcome. I gave forgiveness, showed gratitude, and started the process of letting go of my desire to change her. I softened my tone and told her that she did a great job raising such an ambitious and independent woman. *Like, really great job.* I shouldn't have been surprised that her comeback response was, without any hesitation, "Yeah, I know." This was a classic mom here. "Well, then believe me when I say that just because I didn't need you for this or for that doesn't mean that I don't *need* you, mom."

Once I learned that I had control over my actions, how I wanted to feel, and how I wanted to show up in the world, I started getting myself back. I started realizing that you can't change anyone, no matter how hard you try. It was time to let go and move on before I wasted any more time in this space.

BREAKING THE CYCLE

Kate Northrup, an entrepreneur and best-selling author, provides exceptional tools and resources in her book "Do Less: A Revolutionary Approach to Time and Energy Management for Ambitious Women." She asks us to consider changing our mindset into thinking that one day is always moving toward a new day instead of running out of time in the present day. Where can you start listening to your body, discover your energy and time drains, and learn how to control yourself in a more productive way by doing less? Remember that you are only in control of yourself and your actions. You cannot change anyone! I've tried. So, let me save you the trouble. It is a complete waste of time and energy.

LESSON 6

CHOICES AND BOUNDARIES

Ready to get into some juicy topics? This is where we really start diving into getting unstuck and moving toward creating and living a life you love as the best versions of yourself.

Once we have this increased awareness that an unpleasant situation or feeling is occurring or we are not showing up as our best selves, comes the next crucial decision. Either stay right where you are or choose something different. This choice reveals how we can re-direct this energy into something else, something more positive, more peaceful, and more in alignment with ourselves. You have the control to choose to stay in the unpleasant space of challenge and mindful battle or you can choose anything else. You get to decide your re-direction.

Sarah Blondin is an author, writer, and meditation guide who shares incredible heart-centered wisdom in her book "Heart Minded: How to Hold Yourself and Others in Love." "Door number one is a life full of repeated pain and suffering, the inability to choose otherwise. Door number one is where we stay stuck within our minds, listening to every fear and every worry, as if they are the very reason for our living. Door number two is life that is benevolent and kind, from the moment you first wake. You see things as they are. Reality without condition. You see and understand there is a kindness inherent in everything you get to experiences, and you trust that more than anything else. Your thoughts come and go and fall and rise and you love each one without fight and without war." She goes on to explain how we have a choice every day which door we will walk through. In a soft, nonjudgmental tone, she prays that we wake up from our denial and our habitual, suffering, auto-pilot mind.

This is my absolute favorite topic to talk about when I am giving key-note presentations and it is one of the main reasons behind writing this book. This is when the light bulbs turned on for me and my hope is to encourage a new understanding for you. You see, having awareness is truly the key to self-reflection and self-discovery. Awareness helps make the unknown known. The invisible visible. And once you see it, you have more tools to control it. You are equipped with new knowledge and can take a new direction, a new path, but only if you choose. In "Untethered Soul," Singer tells us that we have a choice to be in full alignment anytime. Let that one sink in, too. It is always your choice.

"In retrospect, dear one, you will understand that your entire life was choices, made one after another in the name of love, or preserving that love," said Sarah Blondin.

WHERE OUR CHOICES COME FROM

Barbara Dossey, Susan Luck, and Bonney Schaub, in their book "Nurse Coaching: Integrative Approaches for Health and Wellbeing," dissect the concepts of "will" and "choices." They state that our "will" is where we direct and harness our energy without any conscious awareness. This contributes to our desired homeostasis and balance, thus determining our conscious choices. So, when we bring awareness to our will, which is present in every decision we make, we can re-write a different ending if we choose. Dossey, Luck, and Schaub describe that our choices typically stem from three different mindsets called willfulness, will-lessness, and willingness.

WILLFUL CHOICES

At the core of willfulness is fear, causing us to make willful choices. Dossey, Luck, and Schaub characterize willfulness in terms of "rigidity and the need to control self and others." This could look comparable to using force to assert power and control by being inflexible, arrogant, manipulative, aggressive, dominating, and self-righteous. My mother seemed to use many examples of willfulness when things seemed out of her control or didn't go her way. In previous lessons, we talked about my mother's judgmental and manipulative willfulness. She always seemed desperate to be right about nearly everything. Even *my* own opinions. She would tell me what I liked and didn't like based on her preferences.

In my young adult years, I remember her asking me what I wanted for my birthday. Usually, I just said some general gift for fear of not wanting to look greedy or fear of her judgments. I never really enjoyed what she got me. Mainly, because it came with some long story of how inexpensive it was or that it was on sale at Hallmark. And it was usually just something she liked, anyway. I never complained. I just accepted the gifts with a smile and shoved it in a closet somewhere. It was just easier this way to try to keep her happy. However, during the infamous year of 2000, I was planning a fun trip to New York City over New Year's Eve with my best friend and really wanted a new camera.

I am about to sound like a dinosaur, but back then we used actual cameras with open rolls of film. So, for my 21st birthday, I asked for a very specific pocket size camera with a new type of cassette film. I gave my mom all the details and even where to buy it. When my birthday came and I opened up the gift, it was a completely different camera! *Are you serious?* It was similar to the one I already owned, just a different version.

The disappointment on my face barely scratched the surface of how I really felt inside. In this moment, I realized how little she heard me in our house. *This was a simple request.* Or so I thought. So I did something I had never really done before. I called her out and questioned her.

"Why did you get this one? This isn't the one I picked out. I was very specific."

"Your dad picked this out," as she diverted the blame to him. Mind you, he had no idea how specific I was because she never told him. I was furious. She added, "Well, you wouldn't have liked that one, and I just figured you didn't really know what you were talking about. This camera is fine."

This points out another concept of willfulness around the desire to dominate. My dad started seeing it too at this point. So, without badmouthing my mom, he returned the camera he bought and brought home the new camera just in time for my trip. These were the pivotal moments in my adult life where I knew there was a disconnect in our realities. These moments started my path of real independence with strength and more certainty. I started deciding what not to do and how I would show up differently in my life. I could see her methods were not working for her, or for me.

WILL-LESS CHOICES

Now, imagine the polar opposite of the willful fighting mind. Dossey, Luck, and Schaub characterize will-lessness with a more passive approach, as an empty feeling. This category reminds me of what I demonstrated more in my teenage and young adult years. This is illustrated as indecisiveness, withdrawal and escape, giving up, distractions, lack of confidence, victim mentality, constant worry, people-pleasing, guilt, and shame. It's not surprising to me that the pendulum swung in the opposite direction for me to compensate for my mother's willful mindset momentum. This was the category I primarily lived in, where my triggers still try to knock on my door to play. I've found that they don't completely go away, but they do get easier with more awareness and resilience.

Through my professional coaching experience, it seemed as if the will-lessness mindset was a common theme among many of my clients. It made me curious to wonder if any of my clients had gone through a similar upbringing with their mother. In addition to the examples shown in previous lessons, here are a few others.

Victim mentality is a self-absorbed mindset that feeds off the self-pity tree and aids will-less reactions. When one lives in the victim mentality, they usually don't see where they have control of their choices. It is a trait where one remains powerless, failing to consider their ability to take action because they may feel it's the only option. There is a lot of blame in victim mentality and feelings that "life" is against them. This is where I hibernated for decades, feeling alone, under her power. It wasn't until I moved out that I realized I had been a slave to her way of life, and I could choose not to be affected by her power anymore. I always realized that an enormous amount of energy went into complaining about our relationships and desperately wanting it to be different.

Distraction is another tactic used to enable will-less reactions. Have you ever set a goal and created the time to allow that goal to happen? Then, when the moment arrived, you distracted yourself with something else? You chose to break that commitment to yourself and fill it with something else. When you did this, you made the decision that something or someone else had more value than the time you finally created for yourself. This is a form of self-sabotage. Instead of valuing your time, keeping a promise to yourself, and taking time to heal, you pushed through for someone else's needs or pure distraction. Or, in my stories, I used distractions to run away from what I really needed to face.

Indecisiveness is the inability to make a decision because there are people-pleasing, constant worry, and feelings of guilt preventing you from moving forward. When you are more worried about what other people will think or what they will say, it's easy to worry that your own decision won't be the right one or may even disappoint someone. You may even stop caring which is you devaluing your opinion or having a lack of confidence in your decisions. As a known peacemaker with my family and friends, this one still manages to creep back into my life. I never wanted to ruffle the feathers.

"Will-lessness is a choice," Dossey, Luck & Schaub remind us. I don't feel that it's always bad, nor am I passing judgment on being will-less; however, just take note of how you feel when you are experiencing it. Ask yourself: is this way of being serving me or holding me back? Sometimes a little is okay, but you decide when enough is enough and when it's time to get out of these passive feelings. Consider how much energy you want (or don't want) to spend living in a will-less state and how much power and control you are allowing it to have on you.

WILLING CHOICES

Willingness is the term used to help us feel more open to new approaches with more flexibility, according to Dossey, Luck, & Schaub. When we turn our attention inward toward ourselves, we are practicing self-reflection. This is the art of understanding how you are feeling and what your physical body is trying to tell you.

This is also the art of diving a little deeper to discover the root cause of our actions and "will." By doing this self-reflection, you are performing a self-assessment check-in.

Pause + Reflect

- ❀ What is out of balance?
- ❀ How does your body feel?
- ❀ Where do you need more love?

CONSIDER YOUR CHOICES

Willingness starts with turning our attention inward and deciphering the facts verses the story you are telling yourself. What are the actual facts here? What are the emotions that you are attaching to exaggerate or change the story? A great example of this was the first time that I failed a test in high school. My mother, trying to console me the best way she knew how, said, "It's okay, maybe you are just not a good test taker." So, at that moment, I decided to make it my true story. I convinced myself that I was just not a good test taker.

But here's the thing: I made that up based on something my mother said *one time*! That was actually not true. The fact was, it happened once, and then I could have moved on and let it go. But I decided to wallow in it and make it my life story for years. The anxiety I gave myself around tests in college became severe. One of the most important tests of my life was the nursing board exam. I was so worried about this test that I gave myself a stress ulcer in my stomach and took anti-anxiety medication the night before the exam. It was brutal and felt paralyzing.

The only real fact was that I failed one test, one time. And the rest was a big, fat, hairy story. I had passed every test after that one in high school. So, I could have written my story instead with, "oh well, happened once, not going to let it happen again," and just brush it off. But I didn't realize I had the power to do that back then.

ACT IN ALIGNMENT

Seeking awareness and getting curious about what's really happening and where you feel these emotions in your body is another key to developing more of a willingness mindset. This comes in handy with worry, anxiety, and feelings of overwhelm. As soon as you have an awareness that you are experiencing these will-less emotions, consider the big picture, or how you want to show up, and work towards taking action in that direction. This continues to be a daily practice for me. I am consistently reflecting on how to show up as the best version of myself and live a life that I deeply love.

SETTING BOUNDARIES

We must consider the ever scary and intimating concept of determining and setting the ground rules for our life, i.e. our boundaries. I define personal boundaries as what's okay and what's not okay, determined only by you and for you. Boundaries are individualized and are not a one-size-fits-all package. We, as a society, are generally not comfortable setting boundaries, especially when other people are involved.

Many view boundaries as a rigid hard wall or just acting selfish. We often share common fears, questioning *what will they think?* Or, we do not want to upset others or make them uneasy. Other common fears around boundaries include abandonment, punishment, or shame. When these fears suffocate our mind, it can lead to avoidance, and more specifically, the inability to receive care or love from others (including ourselves).

Pause + Reflect

- Have you ever allowed behavior that you didn't approve of only to be resentful towards that person?
- Do you consider yourself a people pleaser?
- Have you ever felt taken advantage of?
- Do you feel obligated by guilt and expectations to do things you really don't want to do?

If you answered yes to any or all of these questions, consider that boundaries may be something you would want to start practicing. One of my favorite reads is a book by Henry Cloud and John Townsend titled "Boundaries: When To Say Yes, How To Say No To Take Control of Your Life." They assert that learning how to say no is the most basic boundary because "it lets others know that you exist apart from them and that you are in control of you." Wish I read this one a few decades ago!

A common problem preventing people from setting firm boundaries comes from blaming others for our choices. After reading this book, I realized that I actually did have control over how I wanted my life to look and feel. I started paying attention to people, situations, and experiences that felt toxic to my body. I started imagining what it would be like if I stopped enabling and allowing these behaviors, or even people, into my life. So, of course, I dove deep into my mother-daughter relationship with this one. I asked myself, "What's okay and what's not okay?" I even started to make a list. I was going to break this deep-rooted unhealthy pattern and learn how to set boundaries in a loving and protective way.

I wrote down things that I wanted to stop tolerating. For example, at the top of the list was criticism and manipulative words from my mother. You see, I realized that by tolerating or not setting a boundary, I was essentially enabling her behavior. It felt as if I was giving permission for her to continue treating me this way and talking to me this way. *But this was not okay with me.* I made the decision to set my first real boundary with her sometime in my early 30s.

During our phone conversations, I told her that I was not going to listen to any more criticism or guilt tripping manipulation tactics. I told her how it made me feel and that when it happens again, I will tell her that I love her, but I need to hang up the phone. She was mad at first, which I expected. I mean, her anger was a common emotion, so I was very used to it. So, I started by politely saying, "Mom, I don't like where this is going, I am going to hang up now and talk to you later, I love you." As I hung up, I started feeling FREE! And, even better, her comments and criticisms slowly stopped. I have no clue what was going through her head, but the boundary seemed to work.

I must say, setting that first boundary was the hardest. I pondered over this for weeks before I set it in motion. *What will she think? Will she be mad? It's not worth the fight. It's not going to work. It's only going to blow up in my face.* But when I finally realized that it was ABSOLUTELY NECESSARY, it made perfect sense. Enough was enough, and it was time to stand up for myself and take care of myself.

Boundaries are not selfish if you are loving and straightforward with your approach. Remember, it's about what's okay and what's not okay with you. It has nothing to do with the other person. From this moment on, boundaries became easier and easier the more I realized this was the key to self-love. And, I was a little shocked that it wasn't as debilitating as I thought. We both lived through it just fine – actually, even better than fine!

Creating boundaries with my mother helped our relationship grow stronger. Maybe it was because I started letting go of my emotional attachment and stopped taking things personally. Maybe it was because I decided to not tolerate or enable toxic energies heading my way. Setting boundaries with my own mother made it ten times easier to set boundaries in my personal and professional life. It helped me with confidence and showed others how I would like to be treated and what I deem acceptable. When I set boundaries, I ended my need to people please and tendency to put others' needs and wants about my own.

I continue to learn how to create and teach healthy boundaries for my daughters. I have learned that boundary development in children starts with responsibility and autonomy. "Discipline is an external boundary, designed to develop internal boundaries in our children," said Cloud and Townsend. Discipline should not be considered a punishment but rather teaching that actions have consequences. When the child has responsibility to choose, they have a sense of control and will learn that they can set limits. The earlier children learn this, the more they can learn how to love their choices and decisions. Children need to feel respected and feel comfortable saying no without fear of loss of love. Parents are the role models to teach children to respect the boundaries of others while developing their own internal sense of boundaries.

Cloud and Townsend go on to say, "Boundaries are our way of protecting and safeguarding our souls." Self-reflection is a pure form of curiosity. The curiosity to get to know yourself better by being honest with yourself with full transparency. It is important to get curious about what has been blocking you from creating boundaries in the past and what are your fears about creating them in your future.

Pause + Reflect

- 🦋 What fears or concerns do you have about creating boundaries?
- 🦋 What will people think when you start saying no?
- 🦋 What will happen if you are not so quick to respond to helping others?
- 🦋 Do you think boundaries are selfish? And, if so, how could you reframe your mindset?
- 🦋 Are you ready to create boundaries around people who are draining your time and energy?

CONSIDER YOUR CHOICES

Noticing your own barriers can help you determine how to re-direct. Which brings me to one of my favorite quotes of all time. "Every time you're given a choice between disappointing someone else and disappointing yourself, your duty is to disappoint that someone else. Your job, throughout your entire life, is to disappoint as many people as it takes to avoid disappointing yourself," said author Glennon Doyle, in her book "Untamed."

Wait what? For real? Could it be possible that it is really my duty and responsibility to stay true to myself, value myself, and take care of myself? I feel empowered now when I read this quote and use it often when coaching my clients through boundaries. *Yes!!!! It is my duty and responsibility to TAKE CARE OF MYSELF (mentally, physically, emotionally, and spiritually) even at the cost of disappointing others. Even at the cost of disappointing my mother.*

ACT IN ALIGNMENT

This is where I check in before committing. I ask myself, *am I okay to take this on?* Or, *how am I in this moment? What do I need first?* Like a self-assessment about how full my plate is. Is it overflowing? Or am I okay? Rachel Hollis, in her book, "Girl Wash Your Face" says, "Slow down your YES's and speed up your NO's." This is the key to establishing boundaries with yourself. What does it serve you to constantly keep disappointing yourself? (And then complaining about it or blaming others.)

BREAKING THE CYCLE

My hope is that you are starting to see where our choices come from and how to make conscious decisions to recognize what no longer serves you. At any given moment, you can re-direct your initial choice when you discover that you are going down a path you did not intend. You have control over the words that come out of your mouth. You even have control over your feelings. Remember how you want to show up. What energy do you want to bring to this moment, this day, this life?

Creating boundaries is also a choice. And yes, people may feel upset or disappointed. Can you live with that, knowing that you are making a choice to take better care of yourself? Could you consider this essential to living a life you truly love? "Daring to set boundaries is about having the courage to love ourselves, even when we risk disappointing others," said Brené Brown.

LESSON 7

SHINE YOUR SPARKING LIGHT

This is where the magic starts to happen. This is where we dive into our dreams and find ways to start bringing joy and vitality back to life. Are you ready to create your next chapter? Are you ready to start getting into forward motion into the best versions of yourselves and living your best life? Even if it starts with one teeny tiny step at a time. Come with me on this deeper journey.

VULNERABILITY

When I read about willingness, self-reflection, awareness, and our choices, I can't help but think vulnerability plays a big role. Diving deeper into self-discovery is the true raw form of vulnerability and the key to opening the doors to self-love.

Pause + Reflect

- What do you think about when you hear the word "vulnerability"?
- Does vulnerability feel like a weakness or strength?
- Where are you holding in and protecting your vulnerability?

There are many thoughts, explanations, and definitions of vulnerability. So, I want to take a few minutes and pull back this curtain. Webster's dictionary says vulnerability is the "quality or state of being exposed to the possibility of being attacked or harmed, either physically or emotionally." Other definitions allude that a person who is vulnerable means they are unable to care for or protect themselves, and are easily hurt. If you look up synonyms to vulnerability, most of them were very negative words like exposure, threat, intrusion, liability, susceptibility, and risk. *So wait, being vulnerable is having openness to harm?* If so, I will pass. This sounds consistent with a weak and insecure characteristic that I do not want to be a part of.

In fact, I can guarantee that this was how my mother thought of vulnerability. She couldn't possibly be exposed to her feelings or show any sign of weakness. It would be way too risky. It was a rare sighting to ever see her cry. And, it makes me wonder: is it possible that her dominating characteristics, resentment, and anger covered up any sadness? Maybe anger was seen more as a strength to her, so she displayed that when she felt exposed or too vulnerable. And, if I called her out and questioned why she was angry, it was immediate denial (in a defensive, reactive tone).

If you dive a little deeper, though, you will discover that vulnerability is one step further in a more positive direction than insecurity. Could you consider looking at vulnerability as a sign of "openness" in terms of connecting with others and developing deeper relationships? I have coached many women who may now admit that vulnerability is more of a strength. It's a way to work through challenges and not feel alone. It's a way to develop strong connections with others with feelings of relief and freedom.

"The vulnerability model is a model of understanding the underlying reason for patterns of protective behaviors and the way these set patterns can be obstacles to change," says Schaub in the book "Nurse Coaching." If we can understand why we do things, then we have the power and tools to change. This awareness dives into a deeper understanding of the root cause of our actions and decisions. If we know why we made a certain decision, it can help us validate or find reasons to change our answer if we need to. "Vulnerability sounds like truth and feels like courage. Truth and courage aren't always comfortable, but they're never weakness," said Brené Brown. Can we look at vulnerability through the lens of courage? Courage to open up, take risks, and grow. Because these are more keys to moving forward!

SHARE YOUR GIFTS

Let's peel the layers back and dive into remembering what makes you unique. Put judgment and comparison aside for a few minutes. Reflecting on your gifts, talents, and what lights you up is not arrogant. So do your best not to overthink it. This is meant to see what you really think about yourself. If you are having trouble reflecting on this stage of your life, pick a previous stage or even your childhood era. If you feel ready, take a few deep breaths, and let your mind and spirit run free.

Pause + Reflect

- What do you like the most about yourself?
- What are your strengths?
- What are you *really* good at?
- What brings you the most joy?
- What do you love doing?
- What are your greatest gifts?

Ok a few more deep breaths. How did that go? Was it challenging to think of the answers? If you need more time, come back to this one. These are some of your answers to moving forward when you feel overwhelmed or lost and where positivity and joy come back into your life. Reflect on the amazing things that make you uniquely you. If you still feel stuck on this one, reach out to a few friends or someone you are close with to see what their answers are and compare with your answers. It can be fascinating to see how others view you.

There was a time in my life that, even though I could answer these questions, I had a hard time believing them. Prior to starting my own business, I really felt stuck in my previous job in the nursing profession. For the last two decades, that was all I ever did and all I ever knew. I had always worked in the hospital setting or for a major hospital corporation. For many years, every job I had challenged me, lit me up, gave me joy, a purpose, growth, and showed my strengths. That was until it started feeling stagnant. I never had this feeling before at work. I started feeling bored, unchallenged, and unmotivated. That ugly, negative, convincing self-talk started again: *I have to do this because I am good at it. My family needs the income. It's all I know so why not? I need to work. I am comfortable, and it's safe.* This is what I kept telling myself as I dreaded going into work. I decided to stay safe and comfortably uncomfortable as it started sucking the life out of me.

Here I was, in August of 2018 – we just moved across the country back to my hometown, with a one-year-old baby, new home, new job. I was working to complete my doctorate degree, and even thinking about having another baby. No pressure here at all (*cue a major eye roll*). One day at work, I was searching on the company's intranet and found a wellness section with a link that said, "Get started with a Wellness Coach." The description said that coaches create the space for you to be heard through deep listening without judgment, discover strengths, get unstuck, set healthy boundaries, and positively find your joy in life. *Yes! Sign me up!*

This is when I met my coach, a nurse coach, to be specific. *It can't hurt*, I thought. Our first coaching session was mostly for her to hear my story and what I was searching for. I told her I felt pulled in a million directions yet conflicted with my career choices. I felt overwhelmed and also wanted more, like something was missing. My spark was missing, and I could feel it. The flame was nearly out. She asked questions without judgment, dove deeper into my soul with compassion, and helped bring in different perspectives. It hit me! *This! I love what she was doing for me!* This deeper connection. This is what I love doing with patients, new nurses, friends, and just about anyone. This was one of my strengths and gifts. *And* it had always made me feel good serving in this capacity.

At the end of our first session, she summarized our time together and then asked me to reflect on my biggest takeaways. Right there, with total confidence, I said, "I want your job, I want to be a nurse wellness coach." She almost fell over in her chair, knowing that I couldn't add one more thing to my plate. So, I added, "in three to five years because I need to complete a few things, settle down, and then it's go time." This would be my new chapter, and there was now a new light inside of me. I felt it so deeply that I got started before the three-year mark. I graduated with my Doctor of Nursing Practice in the summer of 2019, when I found out I was pregnant with my second child. The itch for starting the coaching certification program grew, but I knew I needed a little rest first, so I decided to listen to my body. It had been a wild couple of years, and it was time for real reflection before the new baby arrived in the winter. The itch turned into a nudge, hinting "start now because it will take time." I started learning about the programs and decided to begin in April 2020 (with an eight-week-old in my lap).

A beautiful author, podcast host, and friend of mine, Brittany Bacinski, wrote in her book, "All Good JuJu," that "your gifts aren't for you. Everyone's gift, calling and purpose is entirely different. When you become connected with your gifts, you feel in alignment. …and things will make sense. You attract the type of work that your soul wants you to do, the work that is totally removed from ego and totally removed from yourself."

I have finally learned what this means because I can feel it throughout my body. I have finally listened to my calling by looking at my gifts and strengths and realizing how I can best serve in this world. Your gifts are meant to be shared. Consider that by holding them back and locking them down, you are doing a disservice to yourself and to others.

JOY & PLAY

Hard work pays off, *right*? This was a concept that our parents' generation spoke very highly of. There were many expectations around going to college, and the importance of getting a good degree that would lead to a well-paying secure job. Now, I am not completely disagreeing with this concept if it aligns with you and if you have the resources and support. It did for me. I mean my name, Emily, even means hard-working. So, I had to prove it right. I was not afraid of working hard.

For many years, I had two jobs at the same time. As an intensive care unit (ICU) nurse, I also was an adjunct faculty for a nursing school, facilitating students' hospital clinical experiences. Then, when I held a full-time nursing educator job, I also picked up extra nursing shifts at a different hospital, and even some home care nursing as just another side job, *as if that was needed.* My motto was to work hard, play hard. And this did pay off, literally.

But honestly, this became a recipe for disaster and major burnout. I know because I've done it many times. Burnout happens much faster for me now. After having my first child, I scaled back to just one full-time job. But in those first few years of her life, I realized that I didn't want to work this much. With the increased responsibilities at home on top of major life transitions, my body was begging me to slow down.

What I wanted to do was work smarter and play harder! Now, I had many years of this "working hard" scar tissue built up that I needed to chip away at. And trust me, I am still working on this. What I am doing now is checking in with myself by asking, *does this align with where I want to be, what I want to be doing, who I am meant to be serving, and how I want my life to feel?* My nurse coach still connects with me and reminds me to reflect on this every time my ambitious mind gets a new idea. She asks me, "Is this moving closer or further away from your dream?"

Now it's your turn. Time to take a moment to first reflect on what brings you the most joy and happiness. This could be people, situations, events, places, really anything.

Pause + Reflect

- 🦋 Where is your happy place?
- 🦋 What makes you smile?
- 🦋 What makes you genuinely feel alive?
- 🦋 What fuels your soul?

My mother's happy place was around babies and young children. She had so much joy being around kids and genuinely connected with them. This is where my mom's light shined, and it was contagious! Children loved my mom. She volunteered to help at the elementary school in our neighborhood and then became a kindergarten aide. She unquestionably loved "her kids." When she resigned from this type of work, she started helping my friends out with childcare services and became the neighborhood nanny. I will admit, she was pretty darn good! She would get down on the ground and play with children. She had an electric imagination and energy with children. This lesson is one that I have learned to carry with me. This is a part of her that I am most proud of. *Thank you for showing me this side of you, mom.* This was the best version of her (in my opinion).

For eight years, I played very hard. I trained and became an amateur ballroom dancer, inspired by Dancing with the Stars back in 2007. My teacher and I competed pro/am (professional/amateur) all around the United States. In most of our competitions, we even placed in the top three for my age and advanced placement level. It was exhilarating! After about a five year break to get married and have babies, I returned to the dance floor. Not nearly at the speed I trained at before, but it was a step toward bringing joy back into my life and getting lost in play! Being in the moment, through joy and play, can suspend our self-conscious and pause our worrying mind.

TAKING CARE OF YOURSELF

In order to consider how to take care of yourself, it's important to reflect on your feelings around "self-care" first. So, let's start off with a reflection on what self-care really means. And, be 100% honest with yourself here: are you excited about this topic or already rolling your eyes? It's important to dive into this so you know your baseline as we move forward on this journey.

Pause + Reflect

- What do you think of when you hear the term "self-care"?
- Do you think self-care is selfish?
- Is self-care an unattainable, distant thought?
- Do you feel that you have any time for self-care?
- What are your self-imposed barriers towards receiving self-care?

CONSIDER YOUR CHOICES

What came up for you with these questions? Did you have thoughts like, *yeah, sure, self-care is nice in theory, but who really does that?* Or did resentment or envy towards those who practice self-care pop into your brain? Did thoughts about the lack of expenses, lack of time, or lack of energy reveal themselves as barriers to self-care?

Growing up, my mom considered self-care to be completely selfish. By now, you've read examples of where my mom considered healthier behaviors such as boundaries, therapy, and making my own choices as being selfish. Being called selfish was a judgmental term I heard quite often in our home. Remember, earlier I mentioned that she sacrificed her life for her children and wore that badge of honor proudly. It took many years to break this part of the cycle that self-care is not selfish but absolutely essential to my overall health and well-being.

When I was in nursing school and early into my healthcare professional career, I would hear in classes that it is essential to take care of ourselves before caring for others. This made sense to me at the time in my young twenties. How can we think straight and have the energy to care for others if we are exhausted, hungry, and have to go to bathroom? So, early on in my career, I listened to this and made sure I met my basic needs.

However, over time, the demands and stresses of the job increased, on top of having a lack of resources and being short-staffed. It became increasingly difficult to take care of ourselves at work. Many nurses would report never eating, taking a break, or going to the bathroom during a twelve-hour shift! Especially when I worked in the ICU and a patient's blood pressure depended on titrating an intravenous medication just to keep them alive. It doesn't really sound as though I have time to go to the bathroom. "Ask someone for help," you say? That sometimes works, but I usually had at least one other patient to care for and my co-workers were in the same boat.

Talk about feeling guilty. How could I possibly ask someone to watch my patients so that I could take care of myself? This was when the importance of taking care of others before myself became ingrained in my head. Not only did this start to happen at work, but I let it bleed into my personal life, too. I became the self-sacrificing, people pleasing, caregiver, and caretaker of everyone but myself. Especially when I became a mother!

Here was my all-time worst moment. This story is from the early phases of being a new mom, shortly after my first daughter was born. Here I was as a trained ICU nurse educator, having a child of my own. I thought, *if I can do that job, I can certainly take care of a child* (as if that was easier). Don't worry, I am eye rolling myself here.

Was I wrong! I treated everything as if it was an emergency, just like at work in the hospital. And I mean *everything*. I jumped every time she cried. It felt equivalent to a critical alarm going off in a patient room in the hospital. *She needs me,* I thought in extreme panic. There was one night, after she started sleeping in her own crib and room, that we forgot to turn on the baby monitor. So when I heard her, this distant screaming cry, I bolted out of bed in a panic. I ran down the hall, and right before I opened her bedroom door, the worst of the worst happened. Let's just say I forgot to stop at the bathroom first and my pelvic floor dysfunction definitely dysfunctioned on me. Now, I am soaking wet, with a screaming baby in the background, and at a total and complete loss.

Wave that white flag, please. This, to me, was the ultimate need for change. Or at least start with taking the one-minute bathroom break for myself before entering a crying baby's room. *Why didn't anyone tell me it could be like this? Why didn't my mom prepare me for how challenging it may be? Did I seriously accept that I had to take care of everyone and everything else before my own basic needs?* (Insert cry for help here!)

ACT IN ALIGNMENT
Here's the thing: I don't love the term "self-care." Because, for me, it sounded like a luxury day at the spa and something that occurred only on a special occasion. Working in the critical care areas of the hospital had trained me to believe that any amount of self-care (or taking care of myself) came at someone else's expense. I felt guilty for even thinking about taking care of myself when others were in need. This feeling was so strong and debilitating that it blocked me from realizing that I wasn't taking care of myself. It just felt way too selfish to even think about it. *I wonder where I got those thoughts...*

I remember one time, I was daydreaming with my husband about the day I could just lay out at our pool in silence on a floating raft. He laughed, and asked, "In what world do you think that's ever going to happen?" He was right, there just wasn't any time left for this full-time working mom, and I just needed to accept that. Except that my mental health was not okay and was reminded all the time through anxiety, overwhelm, and burned out (or even emptied out) feelings.

But that's when my mind shifted again. That's where the inner child in me brought out the *why not? Why can't I live in that world? Why can't I live in a world where self-care isn't selfish? Why can't I go against the grain to live a life that I truly love?* And, *where do I need to move things around to make that possible for myself?*

I made a decision to shift my negative thoughts on self-care into more positive thoughts about taking care of myself. Just switched the words a little. *Isn't it my responsibility to take care of myself?* It dawned on me. No one is going to take care of me. And I will show up better when I take care of myself. I made the decision to believe that self-care is not a luxury, but instead, an essential piece of survival. Is it possible for you to consider being open and willing to view it differently? Are you trying to just survive this world or actually thrive at the one life we've been given?

Self-care is "a multidimensional, multifaceted process of purposeful engagement in strategies that promote healthy functioning and enhance well-being," said Dorociak, Rupert, Bryant, and Zahniser, in their article titled, "Development of a Self-Care Assessment for Psychologists." What they are saying is that a person makes a decision to act on personal health promotion. They just make a decision? Huh, sounds like we have control over this one. When we lack self-care, research has shown that this can increase anxiety, depression, stress, exhaustion, and burnout. Agreed! So, let's swing that pendulum the other way. When we increase in our self-care or taking care of ourselves, we have improved mood, energy, happiness. Here's the thing, how we view self-care is how we view taking care of ourselves. And this can be a direct reflection on if we are really going to embed it into our lives.

BREAKING THE CYCLE

Now, I am not here to give you the top ten steps to self-care. Because it's no surprise to any of us that eating healthy, exercising, avoiding drugs and alcohol, meditation or prayer, and having support systems are good for our well-being. But you could be doing all these things and still not feeling "well." So, if we know what we need to do to help ourselves and take care of ourselves, why don't we do it? Why do we get stuck and fall back into old patterns?

Understanding and getting to the root of why we aren't doing something reveals the areas of blockage. Is there some scar tissue stories we are telling ourselves that we don't deserve it embedded in guilt with a sprinkle of people pleasing, self-sacrifice, and don't forget, self-sabotage? If this resonates with you, let's dive a little deeper.

Where are you failing to value your needs and putting the needs of others over yours? Sometimes to the point of your own suffering. Is their request or their need really an emergency that trumps your wellbeing? Now, I am not trying to de-value others' needs, but I encourage you to account for where you are at in that moment. Because this repetitive pattern of undervaluing "taking care of yourself" leads to a self-inflicted burnout. Trust me when I say that this is a constant work in progress, but at the core of it is self-love. And by the way, lovingkindness towards yourself is not selfish either. Let's retrain our brain to love ourselves in addition to loving and taking care of others (not either or).

Pause + Reflect

Here is where we start the real daydreaming; one of my favorite things to do. And of course, it starts with self-reflection. Think of the story you want to create and why. Think of an area of your life you wish was simply extraordinary. What does that feel like? What are you doing? Who are you with? I want you to start dreaming big. With no excuses, no barriers, no rationalization. Just visualize your dreams and feel the feelings you experience as you begin to dream big.

- If you could do anything with your life, what would you do?
- What lights you up?
- What dreams did you have as a child?
- What would your next chapter look like and feel like?

CONSIDER YOUR CHOICES

One of my closest friends said to me, "You can't be extraordinary in an ordinary environment." Meaning, if your environment is trying to dull your spark, find a new place. The world needs your gifts. The world needs you to shine. Don't continue hiding behind the curtain. Your butterfly wings are meant to be seen.

I came across a quote from an unknown person on the internet, "I can't settle for just anything. My daughter is watching me." What example would I be setting for them by holding my dreams back and staying stuck? What am I teaching them life would be about? Constant stress, overworking yourself to burnout, getting taken advantage of, and sucking it up, even if you are miserable? *Uh, that sounds just awful.* I know because I did all of that for many years.

Inside, my body was screaming for me to get out of the constant anxiety-ridden, irritable, and stressful state I was living in. I started daydreaming of, "In a perfect world, I would be doing _____ and feel _____." Try it. Actually write it down and time stamp it. You will use this to reflect on at a later time to see if any of your desires came to fruition.

ACT IN ALIGNMENT

I started creating a vision board every year with pictures (and quotes) of what I would project my next year to be in that perfect world. Putting these pictures and thoughts on paper was a way to constantly look at and reflect to see if any were coming true. This kept my dreams visible and a part of my everyday decisions. I would ask myself, were any decisions that I made that day getting me any closer to what's on my vision board? I kept my vision board in a place where I would see every day.

One year, I kept it on my nightstand so that it was the last thing I looked at before bed and the first thing I saw in the morning. This repetitive daily visual was a constant reminder in my brain. It's as though the seeds were planted, and the feelings grew and grew until I acted on them. I have been doing this practice now for three years and each year my vision board came true! *Or did I make it true? Either way,* I thought, *can't go wrong.*

These were all paths in the right direction. So, I felt that I needed to use this tool for growth and reflection. Believing that visualization and manifesting are possible and can work. Now, I will add that once we put it on paper, we also need to let go and trust that what is meant to happen will happen for us. We need to give up a little control and not force it. Plant the seeds, feel the feelings, and let the rest go. As my friend, Lindsey Schwartz, an author, a top podcast host, and the CEO and founder of Powerhouse Women often asks, "What could you do today that would allow a breakthrough in your life?"

EMILY S. JACOBS

LESSON 8

TAKE ACTION

Are you hearing that little whisper to move forward? *Take action…
get unstuck.* Or maybe the whisper turned into a scream by now and
it's jabbing your side, like, "c'mon lady, it's time." You know you
are meant for more than this. You know you are meant to live a life
for you (and not your mom). So regardless of her thoughts, opinions,
or criticisms, what are you waiting for?

Consider how comfortable it can be to stay where you are, even
if it's not ideal. Yep, you heard that right. Many times, we choose
to live in the stagnant discomfort and become familiar with it. It's
almost as if we believe that if we didn't have it, we wouldn't be who
we are. If that's you, just own that. You may still feel that you are
gaining something from staying stuck or choosing not to move
forward. Dig deeper and think about what you are gaining from this
space.

Pause + Reflect

- Is your lack of self-worth telling you that you don't deserve
  something?
- Is it the imposter syndrome telling you that you aren't good
  enough and someone else is doing it better?

- 🦋 Is it the fear of not wanting to take a chance or bet that you can do it?
- 🦋 Is it all the people-pleasing, guilt, shame, overwhelm, lack of control characteristics that are deeply rooted and it's too hard to let go?
- 🦋 Is it thinking that those dreams are too far out of reach?

CONSIDER YOUR CHOICES

If so, reflect on why you are choosing that. But if you are ready to move on, you can decide today to change your direction. You have two choices: settle to stay in your comfort zone (even if you're uncomfortably comfortable here) or be brave enough to see what's on the other side (a little discomfort leading to growth). You have to pick one. Real change can't happen in your comfort zone. Are you ready to start re-writing your new story?

ACT IN ALIGNMENT

The key to moving forward starts with discovering what you really want and why you want that. It is the deep desire that screams at you, "Time to change!" What do you want to optimize in your life right now? It is important to be very clear about these answers, and if you are not, spend a little more time here. Try not to judge or think your answer has to be perfect or good enough. If you are speaking from your heart, it will be. And when you need more clarity, come back to the silence in your heart.

I knew as a young girl that I did not want to depend on anyone to take care of me. Stubborn, yes, but that was me. I didn't want anyone else controlling my life. And I didn't appreciate being told, "no." *I wonder where I got that from.* So, when I graduated from college, I knew it was time to step up to the plate and practice my desired independence. I got an apartment, a job, and started directing money towards paying off my school loan debts. I took every action I could think of to be free and on my own. I knew what the deep-rooted cause was to achieve total independence from my mom. I was going to prove to her and to myself that I could do this, and do it my way, even if it was different than her. I knew from my siblings' experiences that if I ever asked for money, there would be strings attached. *No, thank you.*

About a year after I graduated with my Bachelor of Nursing, I heard about travel nursing. *Wait, what?! Combine my love for work with traveling around the country? Heck yes!* At the time, though, I had a perfectly good job, a great social life, and even started my first real romantic relationship. My life was pretty complete. However, *this* sounded extraordinary. A spark had been lit to take this bold risk. Without hesitation, I signed myself up with my heart pumping with glee as I filled out the applications. The employment contracts consisted of 13-week travel nursing assignments anywhere of your choice throughout the entire United States.

My family and friends thought I was crazy, "Why would you leave all this?" Especially when everything was going so well. Here's the thing: I wasn't running away from anything. I was running toward the life I wanted to create. I had faith that everything would be okay. Actually, I had faith that everything would be amazing. So, as you can imagine, the entire experience was exhilarating. As a 22-year-old woman, moving away from Michigan, I lived in a paid studio apartment in New York City during the beautiful winter holiday months. Was there fear and uncertainty? Maybe a smidge, but not enough to stop me. And this was the first time in my life that I had absolute faith in the process and enjoyed every minute of it. To top it off, I felt proud of myself.

Those three months of my young adult life gave me the confidence to do, accomplish, and complete anything I set my mind to. I remember thinking, if I could do *that*, I could really do anything. So, I came back home for a few months, and then ventured out to Colorado and then Arizona. Faith was the key word here, though. I felt the strong nudges in my body, took action, and had faith in the process with little expectations or fear. There just wasn't room to worry when everything was aligning. My heart agreed.

Now, this is not to say that in the years following, everything was extraordinary from that moment on. Oh no. I previously revealed stories of how I fell into old patterns around self-doubt. Many of those triggers attempted to return, especially with continued criticisms from my mom. So when they came knocking, I occasionally let them back in. I had created this beautiful, exhilarating life for myself and then crashed it with the too-good-to-be-true negative thinking. I am telling you this as a reminder that building resilience is a constant, but essential, component in moving forward. Because every time you try, your old patterns will make that attempt again. When it happens, pull out that Wonder Woman List to remind you what you're capable of and give you strength.

In my early 40s, I took another scary risk when I resigned from the corporate healthcare system. This one took a few years, as there was way more at stake now with a family and house to care for. During those years, I hadn't realized what that nudge was trying to say, except that I was meant for something different, something more in alignment with me. So, I dug deeper into self-reflection using the questions at the beginning of this section. My answers revealed everything around serving in a coaching and mentoring role for nurses, new mothers, wounded daughters... essentially healing the previous versions of myself.

The crazy thing was that I journaled all of this when I first really started feeling stuck three years prior and the answers were similar the second time around. I knew it was the right time now. I could feel it throughout my body and I finally wasn't paralyzed by fear. Now, my logical brain checked out all the plan B's, just in case I failed, which I knew was the wrong mindset, but I couldn't help it. It brought some comfort at the time.

I finally decided to have faith and create a new life as an entrepreneur. I had no idea where this would take me, but I knew it was right for me, and it was time. On my very last day of that corporate leadership role, I felt as though the stars were aligned. It was my sign from God that I made the right decision. Immediately, my body felt free. I felt like I could breathe again. When I removed myself from toxicity; I was able to see clearly. I gave my body and mind the break that I so desperately needed. *I slowed down!* And then, serendipitous things started happening.

On a beautiful fall morning, swaying peacefully on my porch swing, I remember asking God for a sign that everything would okay, even though I already felt it would deep in my heart. I leaned over to readjust my seat and a beautiful butterfly just fluttered out from under the cushion. *Seriously? I mean c'mon!* There honestly could not be a better sign than a butterfly; a pure symbol of expansive transformation and positive change.

The next day, I got a call from the hospital that I resigned from to consult and coach health care professionals on their mental well-being and burnout. Another company even called for the same purpose. At this moment, I started to believe this was not a coincidence. When I chose myself and chose to let go of the outcome, it made way for a beautiful new beginning. And with this new beginning, I developed programs, presentations, and one-on-one coaching to support working moms find themselves again and healthcare givers recover from extreme burnout.

I knew this was what I was meant to do, and yet it took me a while to believe in myself. It took me a while to have faith without certainty. When I reflect on my journals since early childhood, everything I ever wrote about oozed empathy, deep listening, and helping others with this skill. And it was time to really start believing in that. Trusting and believing in myself. I believe that we can't fail at something we are meant to do. Did you hear me? You can't fail at something you were meant to do. We are created for a purpose. I've decided that my purpose is to live a life that I absolutely love while empowering others to do the same by breaking negative cycles. It is possible.

FORWARD THINKING

Now, in order to break out of the comfortable, you need to develop a forward-thinking mindset and a different perspective. Determine why this change is so essential and so important to you. Simon Sinek, author of "Start with Why: How Great Leaders Inspire Everyone to Take Action," reminds us to start every decision by asking ourselves *why*. What is at the heart of this? Why do we believe in it? Your why gives you strength and purpose and this type of energy is what keeps you moving forward. Once you have more clarity on your why, you can begin in the direction you want to take or pursue the goal you want to accomplish.

Have you ever started a goal and then stopped it when it got too uncomfortable? Yes, I'll be the first to admit, this happens almost every time I start a goal or come up with my next plan. Even though I know that if I keep going, I may end up in a different place, a place closer to that desired goal. But it becomes scary. It is usually the scariest the closer I get. So, at that moment, I usually make the decision to let my ego suck me back into my comfort zone. It's okay, we will talk about barriers in the next lesson and how you can just choose to start again.

Gay Hendricks, author of "The Big Leap," discusses how our upper limit is the highest amount of success, love, or abundance that you allow before you start to self-sabotage. This reminds me of that pendulum swing again. Remember when I said that this book was seven years in the making? Well, I had the idea and nudge when I told a few people my stories and they said, "you should write a book." It got me thinking, *maybe I should.*

So, I started jotting down some notes and ideas around the lessons I had learned from my experiences and from my relationship with my mother. I had a feeling back then that I would write a book. I just didn't really *know* it yet. In 2022, I knew it was time and felt that my mother approved. This book would be a love letter to all the daughters (especially mine) to help them feel loved, heard, and inspired.

I invested in a mentor, Lauren Eckhardt, award-winning and best-selling author, and CEO and founder of Burning Soul Collective. I decided to put a little skin in the game, light the fire under my butt, and get moving because I couldn't do this on my own. In her program, the Soulful Author Journey, I decided to take on the 30-Day Writing Challenge with a goal of completing my first draft during that time. My soul was ready to get the words on paper and to be read and hopefully inspire others. At the same time, I invested in another mentor, community builder Lindsey Schwartz, the CEO and founder of Powerhouse Women. What I've since realized, is that I ultimately invested in myself.

Now, I told you I am a recovering perfectionist, right? So, I made the decision that it didn't have to be perfect, just completed. Whatever happens, happens – just start writing. Perfectionism was what was preventing me in the past. This time, I chose to be disciplined and stick to my daily goals. Sometimes, I needed to modify because I became a little rigid or willful, but ultimately with a little grace, I completed it. When I made the decision, reflected on my barriers, and remained committed, the end result is what you are reading right now.

GOALS AND WINS

Keep coming back to your goal, intention, or why you want to get to a more optimal place. Reflect on that small step you can take today. Could you implement this a few days a week or even every day for a few weeks? Remember to start small. Consistency develops habits. Can you commit three weeks of your life? Even if it's a small start to a bigger goal?

I believe in starting with a small goal, one that is achievable but jogs you out of your comfort zone. Remember, a little discomfort is growth, and growth is what makes you move forward and get unstuck. So, think of it this way: a little discomfort every day goes a long way. And then, the magic happens... that discomfort becomes your new comfort. That is a promise.

Pause + Reflect

- Did you decide what you want?
- Is this clear?
- What is the desired response?
- Are you willing to get a little uncomfortable if that meant something better on the other side?

Start with a small goal and see what happens for yourself. Consider one small action step you could start with that would bring you one step closer to your more desired life or a better version of yourself. Be specific. Spend a few more minutes feeling it to be true. Next, decide when you will start this goal. Hint: if the answer is not today or tomorrow, you will want to review why.

- What barriers are in your way?
- Are you really all in, despite any barriers?
- Is this really a burning, deep desire that you want to change?
- What if today was the last day of feeling_____?
- What would that change for you?

Now, the biggest key to this entire journey is consistency and showing up for yourself. Prove to yourself that you are committed to yourself and value your end result. This will build confidence. Do you struggle with confidence? Well, stop breaking promises to yourself for other people. Prove to yourself that you can commit to yourself as you do to others.

🦋 Are these goals getting you closer to that feeling or desired outcome?

🦋 If they are not, how do you modify the goal to be more in line with the desired effect?

🦋 If you are achieving these goals and feeling better, ask yourself, "Now what?" Could you add a little more?

CONSIDER YOUR CHOICES

If you are not achieving these goals, review your barriers or what is blocking you. If the barrier is yourself or your excuses, could you consider an accountability partner or coach to assist? This is especially helpful if you know what you need and just have a little trouble staying on track. I'm happy to be your accountability partner! I also want to add scheduling in intentional rest and rejuvenation so that you don't get burned out. It is possible to overdo it. Trust me, I get so excited when I set a goal that I sometimes obsess and then get overwhelmed. Check in with your rigidity and question if it's causing more harm than good. Listen to your body if you need to rest. However, be mindful of excuses feigning as an intentional reset button. They look different.

ACT IN ALIGNMENT

Here is my favorite part, and in my experience, the most undervalued part: Decide how you will celebrate small wins. What are your markers of celebration? Because this is what maintains the motivation to keep going. Celebrating was another big strength of my mom. Despite the many stories I have shared that seem to contradict this, she also always found a way to let me know she was proud, even if I wasn't, or if I didn't see it to the degree she felt it. You see, when she saw my perfectionism and minimizing, doubting self-talk emerging, she stood up for me.

"Emily, don't be so hard on yourself," she would say, reminding me of my strengths. I also imagine her thinking, *no daughter of mine is going to wallow in self-pity.*

She chose to celebrate through gift-giving, which could explain why gift receiving was always so difficult for me, or even celebrating myself was difficult. It was hard to trust. I don't blame her for this, it's just another area of my own necessary self-reflection.

In 2021, I decided to re-write that story. The first time I intentionally celebrated myself was when I passed my Nurse Coach Board Certification Exam. Honestly, celebrating myself was not in my comfort zone, *at all*. My coaching mentor had asked me how I would celebrate my completion. I hadn't thought about how to celebrate myself for an accomplishment that I was proud of.

So, as I drove home after the examination, I ended up in the Hallmark parking lot. I can honestly say that I don't remember driving there, I just ended up there. *It was my mom's favorite store.* I walked around the store many times before I found the most perfect gift. I purchased the most beautiful card and a little tiny dish that read "PAUSE." This is a common theme in the coaching world and in my personal life. Pause and reflect, *hence the self-reflection questions*. So, I wrapped it, wrote a congratulatory message in the card, and then poured myself a glass of wine while I opened my gift in solitude. It may sound silly, but it was very simple and rewarding. I hold this moment close to my heart and have now found little ways to celebrate my wins.

How will you celebrate your wins? Even if it's a special dessert from your favorite bakery, a night out with a friend, retail therapy, positive affirmation post-it notes, or fancy coffee. Because, well, why not? What's life all about if we aren't celebrating achievements?

BREAKING THE CYCLE

When we are on a mission to be the best version of ourselves or live an extraordinary life, it's important to consider that the energy we put out into the universe is the energy we will receive back. Time to check back in with yourself.

Pause + Reflect

- 🦋 What energy are you bringing forward?
- 🦋 What do you want and are you taking steps forward and making choices to reach it?
- 🦋 Or are you making choices that continue to push it away?

CONSIDER YOUR CHOICES

Typically, whatever you are passionate about is where your soul lives. For me, at least in this moment of my life, it's creating a supportive, loving, trusting, mother daughter relationship with my girls. I am so passionate about learning how to meet them where they are and learning how to parent and discipline while not being too controlling. This is a tough balance for me, but I am grateful to know that I am not doing this alone. I know who my support system is because I've created this tribe. From my friends, family, husband, community, church, and other moms. I have chosen all of them for a reason and I feel that they are all in unapologetic alignment with me. Creating a community of supportive moms through my company has been one of the greatest gifts of my professional life. I provide the space for us to heal together. And it makes my heart burst with love knowing that these moms are creating beautiful relationships with their children while forgiving themselves for not being "perfect."

ACT IN ALIGNMENT

I didn't know this was my passion until I was living in it *every day*. I didn't realize how important breaking the toxic cycles really were until it was my reality and in my face all of the time. *Or did I?* I had lived through one cycle with own mother and knew as a young child that I would create something different for my future family. This was a huge ah-ha moment for me. I remember thinking back to being a young child, knowing deep down in my heart that there would be a different path for me.

You may have heard of the law of attraction from the book "The Secret" by Rhonda Byrne. You attract what you think you deserve (good and bad) based on that energy you put out there. Are you saying you want more but then talking yourself out because you think you deserve less? Thinking and acting in this mindset is a blocker. You attract the right people when you start loving yourself and creating boundaries around the life you want to live and how you want to be treated. Like attracts like. What you are looking for, you have to start displaying, too. And that rings true with celebrating ourselves. It shows our heart that we are worth celebrating and we deserve inward love and attention.

112

LESSON 9

CHANGE YOUR PERSPECTIVE

This is one of the final lessons in taking 100% accountability and ownership in your decisions. But let's face it, you are also going up against the odds. There will be barriers to consider as you begin this new path. It will be essential to line up tools and resources to assist when things get challenging. In order for you to make a breakthrough, the desire to take action and make a change has to be greater than the resistance you will be up against. So, let's reflect and check in on your ownership, barriers, and accountability.

Pause + Reflect

- How committed are you?
- What has prevented you from moving forward in your past?
- What barriers do you foresee with this goal?
- Are you letting external circumstances predict your success? If only _____, then_____.
- Do you lean more on your backup plan?

CONSIDER YOUR CHOICES

Shawn Achor asks, "What is it that won't let us live our lives?" When I hear that, I take a deep breath and get honest with myself.

113

Usually fear, doubt, or uncertainty are one of the answers. So, I dive a little deeper, *fear of what?* Consider if you have a fear of failure or even a fear of success. Yes, it's true. Some people actually fear success. They fear who they become on the other side of facing their fears and self-doubt. They are afraid of meeting that person. *You know, the one they strive to become.* This is why breaking the cycle can be so hard and why we fall back into old patterns.

However, life is meant to progress through learning and growth. When a baby starts learning how to walk, how many times do they fall? As a parent, do you get mad at them? Do they get mad at themselves? *No.* You just encourage them to get back up and keep trying until they get it. If we don't get mad at babies, or other people for that matter, then why the heck do we get so upset with ourselves? We are not perfect, nor will we ever be! End of story. Time to get over that.

ACT IN ALIGNMENT

If you are completely committed to living your life for you (and not your mom, or anyone else), it looks a bit like this: you make a decision to stop putting contingencies on your goals and decisions. You don't wait until everything is perfectly aligned to take action. You won't lean heavily on a back-up plan because then you are directing more energy there. I mean, does a baby have a back-up plan for failing to learn to walk? Sure, they may continue crawling for a bit, but, after falling on their bottoms many times, they learn to work with the discomfort and figure it out. Become comfortable with discomfort, knowing that you are getting closer to your goal.

The remainder of this section will talk about the top three barriers that frequently arise in my coaching practice. My hope is that with an increased awareness and perspective, you may discover tools to re-train your brain in considering these your challenges to overcome over true blocking barriers.

TIME

Let's review the concept of time. *If only I had more time. If only there were more hours in the day. I'm so busy.* Yes, I have complained numerous times about this specific barrier. There never seemed to be enough time for me to create the life that I wanted. I made logical excuses to not create that time, always felt rushed, and always tried to cram so much into a short amount of time.

My mother had a lot of negativity about the present moment of time. She would also say things like, "I never have time for myself. I dedicate all my time to my kids." She said this with pride, because being a martyr was another badge of honor. But what I noticed in her face, tone, and body language was burnout, fatigue, overextending herself, and working so hard to be perfect. Despite what she said, she was not happy in this space. She was not living as her best self. She was not valuing herself. But she would also not admit it, either.

Time is still the biggest barrier that loves to hold a tight grip on me. I used to wear my multi-tasker badge with such pride. Boasting about how much I accomplished in such little time. It became a sport of how much could I squeeze into the time it takes my kids to put their shoes on (empty the dishwasher, start the laundry, etc.). My husband often gives me the look implying "you're doing that *now*?" And truthfully, my response is usually something like, "Yeah, why not? Why wait? I don't have time for waiting." The problem was that, at some point, my body and mind started to suffer from the feelings of overwhelm and burn out.

I felt similar to a super-productive, overzealous, over-achieving wonder woman. I know that I aced this skill from the master herself, *my mother*. This woman made plans about her plans and then more plans on top of those plans. You get the picture. The problem was that I would then complain about rushing, even though I was the one who created that rushed feeling.

Now, I am not saying there is anything wrong with doing things while you are waiting or even multitasking a little. Just consider that this is a form of distraction and actually reduces productivity. And, before you add more to your plate or say yes to one more thing, ask yourself if this will help you or make things worse for you.

Pause + Reflect

- What is your relationship with time?
- Do you feel like there is just not enough time or hours in the day?
- How do you feel talking about time?

🦋 How do you treat time?

CONSIDER YOUR CHOICES

I still continue to fall into these patterns and have to regularly check in with myself. When I feel overwhelmed and stressed (which still happens today) mainly about time, I reflect on a few questions. *Where am I not prioritizing my end result or how I want to feel?* For example, if my goal was more patience and peace, then *am I taking actions towards that goal or away from it? Where do I need to modify my calendar and move things around to make time for what I need (big picture)? How can I have a better relationship with time?*

Not like in a fairytale land, but realistically. Listen, I am not saying that this is easy, but it sure does seem necessary. At least this one did to my mental health. And, as a mother, I have realized this mindset was most likely passed on from generations and that I needed to change this destructive pattern and role model differently for my daughters.

The majority of women I coach also talk about time negatively – mainly that there is just not enough. "I wish I had more time for this," and, "if only I had more time, I would do that." Other comments are complaints about rushing time or desires to live in past times. And, the number one thing I hear is, "I never have any time for myself. I do everything for everyone else, and there is just no time left for me." Typically, when I dive deeper, the guilt stories come in.

Women are reporting to me constantly that they feel guilty for taking any amount of time for themselves, especially working women. But here's the thing: you can't pour from an empty cup. If the tank is empty, the car won't drive. Even just a little gas (or small amount of time) may help you reset, have more energy or be in a better mood, or show up as a better version of yourself. When there is nothing left, we feel lost, hopeless, and like a martyr. I can't imagine we want to teach our children to run themselves into the ground and burn themselves out repeatedly, for the sake of others.

ACT IN ALIGNMENT

You are the owner of your time. You heard that right. You are the creator and owner of your time. We all have the same 24 hours in a day. All of us! No more and no less. I know you can think of judgmental examples where you've said, "How does she have the time for that?" She created it. And shocker alert: YOU CAN, TOO!

Concept of Time Experiment
Based on author Eve Rodsky's book "Fair Play."

For one week, calculate the average number of hours that you think it takes to do your everyday tasks. I am going to show you by using an example of a full-time working mom with kids in either school or daycare.

Sleep: Ideally 8 hours each night = 56 hours/week

Grooming: 1 hour per day (includes a nighttime routine) = 7 hours/week

Morning routine with kids: 30 minutes a day = 3.5 hours/week

Bedtime routine with kids: 30 minutes a day = 3.5 hours/week

Meal prep and cleanup: 3 meals a day (including packing lunches) at 1 hour each = 21 hours/week

Mealtime: 21 meals at 30 minutes each = 10.5 hours/week

Work: ideally 40 hours per week (I know that this will vary) = 40 hours/week

Drive time to work and childcare: average 1 hour round trip = 5 hours/week

Grocery shopping: 2 times a week = 2 hours/week

Domestic household tasks: average 1 hour each day (cleaning, laundry, or other) = 7 hrs/week

Total = approximately 155 hours. So, if there are 168 total hours in a week, this leaves 13 hours a week left for any quality time, extracurricular activities, down-time, me-time, buffer time, self-care, etc. Now, run this experiment in your own situation. Calculate your time as realistically as you can.

Pause + Reflect

🦋 What is your number left over?

🦋 How will you use the remaining hours?

🦋 How will you fill this time?

🦋 What is your perception of the time leftover? Is it more than you thought? Is it less than you need?

- What are your feelings around it?
- Are you living in the comparison of Who's Busier Olympic Games?
- How can you tweak ways to make this more realistic for you?
- Where can you find ways to create more time for yourself or doing things that really matter to you?
- What are your key priorities and how do you create more time for that?
- What can you outsource?
- Where can you look outside the box?
- Where can you change your mindset to knowing that you are the creator of your own time?
- Where can you shift from *finding* more time to *creating* more time?

CONSIDER YOUR CHOICES

You will never *find* time. Time is not lost; it's right there, waiting for you to use it wisely. Hendricks in "The Big Leap," states that "You are where time comes from." He goes on to explain how to take charge of your time so that you are "living in Einstein time." This starts with limiting the energy draining activities that are sucking the life out of you. When you act as though there is not enough time, everything seems urgent.

I actually worked really hard on a goal to create a little more time for myself for "self-care." Guess what I did next. Self-sabotaged it by making myself busy, finding things to do around the house, and distracting myself. *I should be doing laundry, cleaning, anything on my to-do list.* It was only 30 minutes that I carved out and I couldn't even stick to my small goal. Talk about loss of confidence in myself to follow through. This happens to a lot of people. Once we create that time for ourselves, our guilt sucks us back, telling us we don't deserve that time.

This goes for professional work, too. I had many nursing educator colleagues and healthcare professional clients who would talk about being overwhelmed with the amount of work on their plate, staying late to get more work done, never leaving on time, never taking a break, feeling guilty leaving work undone, and without a doubt burning themselves out. So I dug a little deeper and realized they felt as if they had lost their sense of control. They didn't want to speak up or stand up for themselves for fear their boss would be disappointed or fear of losing their job. They were trying to prove to themselves that everything was fine and they could keep pushing through it. But at some point, that false optimism morphs into pure defeat. They chose to devalue their time, health, and life.

I also want to point out that living in a state of "lack" and a complaining mindset only blocks you from any chance of moving forward. If you never feel like you have enough time, you never will. Consider that what you put out there is what you will receive back. So, "there's never enough time" will continue to knock at your door and try to tear you away from your goals or desires if you continue to let it in. Try to find ways to prove yourself wrong. If you complain about not having enough time, but still choose to make yourself so busy that you won't ever have it, that tip is for you. You're not alone – I have easily done this to myself!

Consider all the times you thought or said, "I ran out of time," or "there is not enough time." When you tell yourself this, you are giving *time* control over your life and playing the victim to time. It's TIME to stop letting your issues with TIME control you. When you feel lack, you live in lack. How can you change your perspective and choose how you talk about time and how you spend your time?

ACT IN ALIGNMENT

When I was a single woman in my 30s, I remember telling my brother that I would love to go to church but just don't know if I have time. He quickly responded with, "If you want to go that bad, you will make the time." *Yes, that's right.* I can make that choice and I can make that happen or just continue complaining about something that I say I want but taking zero action. *Who's stopping me? Time? Huh*, in a comedic voice I remember thinking, *time to look at myself and my priorities.*

The other point that I want to drive home is that "busy" is a word that means excessively occupied. Do you see that word "excessive"? Do you love hearing about how busy and exhausted everyone is? Do you love telling stories about how busy you are and all the circles you run in all day long? Are you exhausted in your own business? "You are in charge of your own life, sister, and there's not one thing in it that you're not allowing to be there," Hollis said. Consider putting more value toward your own time and energy.

MONEY

Money is also often viewed as another negative barrier and perceived as a scarce resource. "If only I had more money, I could do this or that." If you think there isn't enough, there will never be enough. Now, I am very realistic with this one and love to budget and be logical, too. So, it's important to dive deeper into the reflection questions about your feelings around money. I also want to take into consideration that things cost money, too. However, regardless of your socioeconomic background, you can still reflect and find alignment with the choices you have control of.

Pause + Reflect

- What is your relationship with money?
- How do you feel talking about money?
- How do you treat money?

CONSIDER YOUR CHOICES

I have heard very wealthy people make the statement, "if only I had more money," as they work excessive hours putting their health at risk. I consider this living trapped in a poor man's mindset. I've heard them complain, stress, undervalue, and underutilize what they have. Frugal and sensible is one thing, but restrictive, cheap, and complaining is a whole other ball game. It's exhausting to hear. I would know, because I've been there and I've done that, too! I was one of those people. And, let me fill you in, it doesn't feel good living in this space.

When I was a young kid, my parents taught me some very great lessons about saving money. My father's thought process was that when I made money babysitting, walking dogs, and extra chores around the house, that I should put away half into a savings account that I wouldn't spend. Although he didn't explain it this way, I interpreted it to mean, "put it away and pretend it doesn't exist." So, that's exactly what I did for many, many years. In fact, I acted as if I didn't have that money. Although, I believe this was a good lesson as a kid, it had a negative effect on my adult money mindset.

It later turned into feeling as if money controlled me. Every decision I made had to do with money. If I spent money, there would be less to save. Yet it remained stagnant in an account, doing absolutely nothing for me. It sounds silly, but it was actually causing stress. *I know. I hear you.* I told myself that I was just frugal, but the truth is that I had a hard time spending money on myself. Anytime I did, there was an enormous amount of time rationalizing, judging, and justification. *Was this related to my parents' poor-man-syndrome talk in the house?* My mom always made it seem like there wasn't enough and comparing it with what others had. Mind you, we seemed to have enough.

Picking up ballroom dancing was my first major financial investment into myself, which ended up pulling me out of depression. *Pretty decent return on investment there*! In my early 30's, I purchased my first home on my own with only a small amount of buyer's remorse. This was liberating for me!

In my early 40's, my dad and I were talking about something related to money and he just nonchalantly mentions that he was never really good at spending money. That he really didn't know how to do it and never felt comfortable spending it. He also mentioned that my mom did all that for him. *What?! Are you for real? How did I not know this?* Huge light bulb moment. My entire relationship with money came full circle in this one conversation. I had been living in poor man syndrome and paralyzed myself for years when it came to money. I had no idea my dad had a hard time with this, too.

So, no one really taught either one of us how to enjoy the money we earned? Every dollar was justified. And we both had difficulty spending! I wish we would have talked about this, earlier. I wish I would have known this about him. I may not have felt so alone in this mindset.

ACT IN ALIGNMENT

I am not saying that saving is bad, just check in with the feelings you are attaching to money. For me, there just wasn't a healthy balance, and it prevented me from enjoying it. I worked hard collecting it and then placed it in a dark box. It was time to let it breathe. Amanda Frances, author of "Rich as F*ck: More Money Than You Know What To Do With," says that we need to tell money how to serve us. Give it a job. Decide how money will act in your favor.

I will say that I finally started getting more comfortable spending money, investing in my business, my children, my home, and myself. I've learned to see money as serving me and show gratitude for the ways in which it does. I started allocating money and giving it an assignment so that it could find ways to serve me abundantly.

A percentage would be for saving, similar to a one-way street. But this time, I didn't pretend that it didn't exist. It had a very important purpose: retirement and emergencies. It would take care of us when we absolutely needed it. Next, I would allocate a percentage for the cost of living (house, car, groceries, bills, etc.). Next, educational expenses for my children. Next, for business expenses and savings. And last, a personal account to invest in myself. This was an account that I never really had. A percentage of money that I could do whatever the heck I wanted without any guilt or justification. I felt as though I could breathe again. I used this account to re-invest in myself by reenrolling in ballroom dance classes, picking up business mentors, and pursuing personal growth.

I believe that by spending money with thoughtful and beautiful intention, it has given back to me 100x! It has never failed me; this practice always took care of me. Money doesn't want to be kept in a dark box. It needs to be given a purpose. I didn't know money could do that, but let me tell you, this worked for me.

Where can you begin to look at your finances differently and develop a better relationship with money? Authors Dethmer, Chapman, and Klemp, in their book "The 15 Commitments of Conscious Leadership," say that "scarcity belief that there is not enough" causes us to be driven by fear and focus our thinking in the wrong direction. Consider how you want money to work for you and serve you in a more strategic and beautiful way.

SELF-DOUBT

If it isn't money, and it isn't time, maybe it's *you* you'll need to stand up to. Maybe you are your biggest barrier. This is such a tough pill to swallow. I know this one, too. I became comfortable in a stagnant place, developing more and more scar tissues, and turning these into my excuses to break the cycle. These excuses were driven by the fear infecting my mind. We covered self-doubt early on; here is where you have the choice to come full circle and unwind what is blocking you from moving forward. Listen to your heart's desire.

Pause + Reflect

- Are you scared of what you can actually achieve?
- Do you fear succeeding? Yes, this is actually a thing!
- Are you talking yourself out and making excuses?
- Do you gain empathy from pity?

CONSIDER YOUR CHOICES

If you are the one making your decisions, then you have the power to change your story. Indecision or inability to move forward is playing it safe and familiar. Do you continue to complain about it and choose to not change anything? Think back to the self-sabotaging upper limit references. Hendricks asserts the reason we can't expand to our fullest potential is because of our self-limiting beliefs. Worry and anxiety block our positive flow of energy, which in turn, decreases our integrity. Here is where those nasty fears arise: fear of failure, fear of disappointment, and fear of success.

I've said it before and I will say it again: self-doubt and devaluing yourself leads to overwhelm and emotional burnout. Do you disagree? Or, can you at least agree that self-doubt doesn't get you closer to your goals or getting out of this toxic feeling?

ACT IN ALIGNMENT

I've learned through research and my own history how to turn my anxiety into a lesson. Dare I say, a gift. *Ugh, that was painful to say.* And yes, I still have anxiety from time to time. But I do my best each time to realize that it's a signal that I'm out of alignment with what I deeply desire. When it happens, I feel the volcano about to explode over the littlest things (or at least it seems little upon further reflection). Most of my anxiety came around time and money. Which for me, if I am the creator of my time and money, then I contribute to and create my anxiety. *Ouch.* This still hurts, but it's a reality for me. I was blocking myself from receiving the beautiful gifts that time and money can serve me.

I started with learning to create a better relationship with my own anxiety. Every time it comes knocking at my door, I quickly pause and reflect inward. *How is this serving me at this moment?* (Hint, it's not, and I'm getting caught up in the control cycle again). Then I ask, *how do I want to show up? Well, not like a crazy lunatic...* so I take a deep breath and try to reset. That quick pause, every time, helped build up my resiliency muscle.

Now, I'm not perfect. Every once in a while the volcano explodes, but with accountability I get back on the "all in" wagon and each time is getting shorter and easier. Now, that's my personal story. I am not trying to solve everyone's challenges with a magic wand. And, if you need medical attention, please seek it. But at the same time, get curious about the anxiety, too. I also discovered that coffee was contributing to my morning anxiety and did not help my time anxiety getting the girls out the door for school. So... this coffee lover decided to take on a 30-day challenge and see if eliminating coffee would bring me more peace and help me show up better for my family. This wasn't easy, as we designed the dining room in our home into a coffee shop and my husband makes the most amazing lattes, but a few days in, everyone noticed the difference, especially me.

BREAKING THE CYCLE

Are you going to accept what life hands you or are you going to start creating your own life? Mary Oliver, in her poem, "The Summer Day," asks, tell me, what is it you plan to do with your one wild and precious life?" You know change is uncomfortable. Think about the transformation that a butterfly goes through; shedding old layers prior to an exhilarating and beautiful rebirth.

Well, is it possible that you can get comfortable with a little discomfort? Is it possible to let go of the tight control you have on comfort? And make a decision that when it gets uncomfortable you will keep going? Otherwise, you just signed up to try, and that won't get you anywhere. Trying just says that you aren't fully committed but still want credit.

Now, the lesson I learned from my mom with all of these barriers, which I mentioned before, was not to control the situation or manipulate people. Whenever she did that, it usually backfired on her and made things worse. Check in on your intentions and what you really want to get out of it. Even if you don't like the answer, be honest with yourself. If your intentions suck you back into the negative, work on these first. If you get stuck on self-doubt, pull out your Wonder Woman list and keep it close. Read it when you are ready to give up on your goals.

If you've read this far, you have probably learned a few new things. And guess what? Once you learn something, you can't unlearn it. That's right. Congratulations! All of these lessons are now in your bucket of knowledge. Ready to get out of the negative and start focusing on the positive to reach what you are capable of?

Pause + Reflect

- Could you have grace with yourself in the process and learn to expect that barriers will arise?
- Can you decide what tools you will utilize when the barrier shows its face?
- Could you consider the barrier more like a lesson to learn?
- Can you look at barriers like feedback and a challenge to see how committed you are?

CONSIDER YOUR CHOICES

Be okay with discomfort. Be okay with disappointment. But stop trying to convince yourself that life is fine the way it is, especially if it is not for you. Especially if you feel that you are meant for more. Winston Churchill once said, "Success consists of going from failure to failure without the loss of enthusiasm." Failure is just feedback to do things differently next time. Pay attention to the thoughts that oppose what you really want. Thoughts are similar to seeds and your subconscious takes everything so seriously.

ACT IN ALIGNMENT

Your mind actually doesn't know what is even real, it just knows what you feed it. These negative, self-doubting thoughts are bringing up the triggers around your unresolved issues and do not have to be a part of who you are and the best version of yourself. Get curious about what thoughts you feed your mind and what you believe. And remember, you have already learned that keeping promises to yourself increases confidence. So, what could you start deciding for yourself today?

LESSON 10

ACCEPTANCE, FORGIVENESS, AND GRATITUDE

ACCEPTANCE

For over 20 years, I had tried to change my mother or wish she was someone different. Two years before her unexpected death, I learned these final lessons, which started to free me from so many of those drowning traits. You've realized by now that we learn behaviors passed down through the generations and, at the same time, we have the power to change these with our own thoughts and actions.

My mother had a hard time letting the past go. She carried so much energy around her love of the "good ol' days" that she became obsessed replicating old memories to fill that missing piece of her heart. For example, she enjoyed recreating the same pictures with each new grandchild that arrived. This was sweet at first, until it became forced with her unwanted requests to recreate almost every memory exactly the same. She had over 100 photo albums of her children and grandchildren. Again, this brought her so much joy but at the same time, it clouded the present moment.

Over time, it didn't allow space to create fresh memories. She was so attached to the past that she could not find happiness in the present and always complained about the way things were today. This was a huge lesson that I learned from her. We cannot change or recreate the past. And the more we try, the harder it feels emotionally. Like an immense weight that we can't move. And we have to accept it.

What I did love about my mother, was that she oozed vitality in her spirit. My mom was an energetic, passionate ball of fire. You could feel her presence in a room (good and bad). Her laughter was loud, her compassion was full, and the love in her heart was genuine. Just ask her "fan club." This was the term she gave to her trusted tribe of friends. Most of them oozed the same zest for life, and it was fun to watch them get together. It was so great to see my mom surrounded by her people without judgment, one upping, or comparisons. Just being.

When I learned to accept her and not try to change her, my heart changed. It started opening up to the possibility that we could co-exist this way. It gave me permission to live in alignment with myself, and that there is more than one way to live in this life. I gave up on spending energy trying to control our relationship and our situation and just let it be. There was positively nothing I could do to change her, and that was that.

As you can imagine, this did not happen overnight and it took years for me to strengthen this muscle. I wholeheartedly believe that she did the best she could. Even though she was different from what I wanted in a mother, I learned to accept her for who she was, and that made me stronger. She, unknowingly, pushed me right out of the comfort zone she was trying to create for me. By accepting this, and accepting her, it allowed me to move forward on my own time and on my own terms. *Just the way I wanted it.*

FORGIVENESS

The concept of forgiveness and letting go starts the true, long-lasting healing journey. This applies to forgiving others, forgiving situations, and especially, forgiving yourself. Remember when I said "what happened, happened"? I meant that. What's done is done, and you can only move forward. Let's start with an awareness of forgiveness and start taking responsibility to move forward.

Pause + Reflect

- ✈ Where in your life do you need to practice forgiveness towards others?
- ✈ Where in your life do you need to practice more forgiveness towards yourself?
- ✈ Can you at least see that by not forgiving yourself, you are holding on to the part of your story that you are not willing to let go of?

CONSIDER YOUR CHOICES

My brother taught me that forgiveness does not mean you forget what happened. It just means that whatever it is stops having control over you. Well, I let go of control and stopped trying to change my mom. Then came the hard part, learning how to forgive the past and move forward. Over those two decades, and after every argument, my internal family would spend an enormous time debriefing about what just transpired. Most of the time we were trying to justify her irrational behavior, unkind comments, self-righteousness, condescending attitude, and manipulative, controlling mindset.

Sometimes, we would even excuse the behavior with, "she has a good heart," or, "her heart is in the right place." We all realized that the way she was brought up may have set her up for having these traits. But it was still no excuse for her behavior or lack of realizing the effect she had on us. Big picture, though, her methods were not working for the family she created. This was probably the largest disconnected piece to understanding our family puzzle.

ACT IN ALIGNMENT

Choosing forgiveness opens up space in your heart for more things that bring you joy and peace. I chose to forgive my mother and chose to believe that she did the best she could. I chose to stop blaming her. I chose to not let her way of being dictate mine.

I am going to take forgiveness one step further by asking you to reflect on yourself. Lean in to where you are being unforgiving towards yourself. Remember that it can be easier to give forgiveness toward others. However, self-forgiveness is the genuine challenge to breaking free from our unhealed past.

Pause + Reflect

- What do you need to forgive yourself for?
- What part of your character do you wish you had less of?
- What part of your personality do you wish you had more of?
- Where can you ease up and find grace in yourself?

Here's *my* crazy answer. I realized that I needed to own my self-inflicted stress. Like, really own it. I am not saying the circumstances that happened in the past were okay; I am just working on this present moment and how to move forward. I had created everything that I ever wanted and could dream of in my life, yet I had a hard time letting go of that chaotic feeling. As part of my daily routine, I was holding onto anxiety and stress because that is what I was used to. It was so deeply embedded that I unconsciously found moments where I created more stress when there wasn't enough. *What?!* Sounds weird, but with deeper reflection, I found this to be true.

Pretty much every Christmas at my parents' house was filled with some joy sprinkled with a ton of stress, pressure, and unease. The constant feeling of "so much to do and so little time." My mother so deeply wore herself out preparing that she was overly exhausted and irritable when the time came for joy and celebration. Every little thing would bother her. Between my brothers and I, we would joke every year, "Who's going to ruin Christmas this year?" Because, in her eyes, there was always someone else to blame for causing her negative behavior. This was especially true when we started having families of our own, and were interested in creating some new traditions.

Fast forward to our first Christmas after she passed, when I decided to host it at my new house. Everything was easy and peaceful and joyful, yet my brain tried to create more stress with the desire to control everything. It was painful trying to stop it. I kept telling myself, *seriously Emily, like we really need THAT energy around this holiday... her favorite holiday.* Now, with the resilience muscle built up and lessons already learned, I was able to calm that controlling mindset down every moment it tried to creep back in. But not without a challenge.

What I'm trying to say is that we can't stop the triggers from happening, but we can choose to not allow them inside and completely take over. Anxiety was a part of me and at the same time it was my responsibility to work with it, not against it. All of this started with having grace and self-forgiveness. I had to give myself permission to let go of the chokehold anxiety had on me. *Seriously, though, what was being so hard on myself actually serving? Where can I have grace with the past and find strength for the future?* In order for me to be the best next level version of myself, I had to lay to rest this version of my story that no longer served me.

GRATITUDE

I want to end with something that I really could have started with: gratitude. Living with gratitude is the first place to start believing that you are capable and abundant. You have two choices here: live in the mindset of scarcity, lack of, or never enough, *or* believe that you have everything you need, you are exactly where you are supposed to be, and that you have more than enough. It's so easy to fall into the pitfalls of lack and focusing on what we don't have, but think about what this state of mind gives you and what it costs you.

Pause + Reflect

- ❧ Which frame of mind feels better to live in?
- ❧ Which one do you believe is true or desire to be true?
- ❧ Where do you feel negativity is weighing you down?
- ❧ Where do you feel any sort of lack?
- ❧ Where can you start to shift this mindset into knowing this is all a perception and you can create a new reality?

Now let's take this a step further. Think back to when you hoped, dreamed, wished for something that you currently have now.

Now, think about what it was like before you had that. Do you remember your feelings? Reflect on any negative self-talk thoughts or if you ever tried to talk yourself out of that goal or dream.

And lastly, reflect on where would you be now if you hadn't had, done, or completed that.

Now, consider looking at this example with more gratitude.

CONSIDER YOUR CHOICES

This is the mindset shift and re-direct that you have been reading about throughout this book. Thoughts are just triggers to see what direction we will go in. The opposite of feeling overwhelmed is the feeling of gratitude and abundance. Typically, when I am overwhelmed, it's because I am ungrateful for where I am in that moment or what's going on. And, the crazy thing is that I previously prayed and hoped for the exact thing making me overwhelmed in the present moment. So, did I pray to be overwhelmed? *Of course not.* But could I look at it through different lenses? Business strategist Jasmine Star wonders if the feeling of overwhelm is simply the abundance of what we once prayed for.

Most of the time my mom seemed to live in a lack mindset. She lived in the thoughts of never having enough, comparisons, jealousy, envy, and a lot of complaining. I would hear this almost every day and wonder why this controlling woman wasn't finding her way into a better mindset or creating a better situation for herself. She must have just believed that it served her better living here. For the rest of us, it became white noise.

What this taught me was the exact opposite. I learned that if I wanted something enough, I had to show gratitude for what I currently had, otherwise why would I deserve anything more? "Gratitude will shift you to a higher frequency, and you will attract much better things," said Rhonda Byrne. If you are a parent and all you heard were complaints from your children, what does it do to shower them with more rewards? Let that one simmer for a little while. I also learned that if I really wanted something to change, I had to take action consistently and show up for myself.

As a child, I remember usually feeling grateful for everything that I had. Sure, did I wish for a few other things? Yes, but not without realizing that things could have been worse and that I didn't want to take for granted what was already in my life. Remember the story of how I hoped and wanted to be a mother for a very long time? So, when it wasn't going in that direction in my past relationships, I pushed, pulled, screamed, and tried to force it harder. I was trying so hard externally that I neglected to see how much inner work was needed.

So, after about a decade of this tactic *not* working, I decided to let it go. Not give up, but just release the pressure. I basically did the opposite, which was to spend time in the most important relationship... the one I had with myself. *Who am I? What do I like? Who do I want to be around? What brings me joy?* I stopped fighting it. At first, it was painfully uncomfortable. I had never been here before. I had never learned to really get to know myself or considered the path God chose for me. I started trusting that I was okay and exactly where I was meant to be.

Now, I never gave up on the dream of having children. I just paused and changed the way I went about it. I started having faith that everything would work out and there was no more space in my brain to force it. I had nothing to lose here. *Nothing.* In fact, what I gained was self-confidence, independence, joy, and a vision of how I wanted to show up in the world.

What can you be grateful for today?

Who can you thank today? Like for real, stop, get out your phone, and text someone.

I want to mention one more thing about that story. When I was ready to start dating again, I was at my highest vibrational energy, and that allowed me to attract the same. I met my now husband during that time. The crazy thing was that he was the opposite of anyone I dated in the past. He was secure, confident, decisive, strong, honest, direct, took chances, and did not settle for anything in life. He worked hard and when things didn't align, he changed them. He was the opposite of what I expected and everything I needed. My former self would have never picked this man as my partner. And yet, even though it's not sunshine and roses every day, I thank God for him. He is the yin to my crazy yang and the true balance that was needed in my life.

ACT IN ALIGNMENT

Eckart Tolle, an author and teacher, said, "Acknowledging the good that you already have in your life is the foundation for all abundance." If you are curious, I have another exercise you could start doing today. This is a simple daily practice to get your mindset thinking in a more gratitude-abundant state. Get a notebook or something to write on and jot down three different things that you are grateful for daily. You could choose to do this activity in the morning or in the evening. When you start or end your day in a place of gratitude, it fills your body with positivity. When you think, write, or read about your gratitude, your body starts to feel the gratitude all over again. So, it's like a double dose of gratitude. And this doesn't take a lot of time. And lastly, I want to ask you this question right now. Be straight out honest with yourself. Can you be grateful for who you are and how far you've come today? Because you should only be working on making yourself better than yesterday.

BREAKING THE CYCLE

This lesson is meant to provide you with a few tools to change your mindset when it's weighing heavy. My hope is that after deeper reflection and new considerations, you have an awareness of how you want to show up differently and more positively for yourself. Remember that you can't change what happened in the past, but you can re-direct your energies into the version of yourself that feels better. This is a constant practice. This is available to you anytime you start heading down a path that no longer serves you. Each time you bring awareness to an old pattern, reflect on your tools, consider your choices, and decide a route more in alignment.

CONCLUSION

LIVE YOUR LIFE FOR YOU (NOT YOUR MOM)

Why is it that when someone close to us passes away, we start seeing them in a different light? Michael Singer says, "Death is the greatest teacher in all of life." He goes on to say, "While someone could remind you of the insignificance of the things that you cling to, death takes them all away in a second." One of the biggest realizations that I've experienced recently is that most of us live as though life is infinite. More specifically, time is infinite.

Now, I'm not suggesting that we live as though we are going to die tomorrow. However, consider what would you change if you believed that life was more finite instead of infinite? These reflections help us begin to discover our biggest values and major priorities. We do not have to wait until we are on death's doorstep to start to question what we are so worried about and what is the big picture here.

Pause + Reflect

- What is the legacy you want to leave behind?
- What part of you has to die because it no longer serves the life you want to live?

- Is the future self you are dreaming about the person you are today?
- If not, what needs to change?
- Would your younger self be proud of the person you are today?

CONSIDER YOUR CHOICES

These are the reflections that reveal to us how important our choices really are. It was clear to me that my mother was never taught self-reflection, self-love, or self-worth. It appears to me that this would have all been considered selfish to her and maybe other mothers of her generation. Back then, society taught mothers of that generation to sacrifice themselves. I remember her saying, "That's just what you have to do." Although I agree to a certain extent, I believe this mindset set her up to believe that everything else would be considered selfish, even taking care of herself, or living a life she really loved.

So, instead of looking at motherhood as strictly sacrificial, the way she did, could you consider thinking of motherhood as the greatest honor and privilege? I realize that many moments are tough, and many seem like a sacrifice. However, see how you can change your mindset and change your story around it so that you don't lose yourself in the process. but YOU were chosen to have these children. What would change if you started thinking of it more in this light?

As hard as it was to have empathy for my mother all those years, it is very clear to me now. I honestly do realize that my mom did the best she could with the resources and tools she had been given. However, I decided to stop adopting her unhealed patterns as my life story. This is the act of breaking the cycle of destructive patterns. This was the end of that bloodline for me. I made a commitment to show up differently for my daughters.

ACT IN ALIGNMENT

Without all of these stories and experiences, I would not be the woman I am today, nor would I have learned what it takes to stop negative toxic cycles. Thank you, mom, for giving me these experiences so that I could learn how to heal my own heart. I see these lessons more as gifts now. Very uncomfortable, eye-opening, challenging gifts, but still gifts. What my mother really taught me was that it was ultimately always *my responsibility* to take care of myself.

I have learned that when I see toxic energy or negative characteristics coming back to play, I am not consumed by them and can divert them at any time. I do not need to give them the power over me. I value myself so much more now. Because of my experiences and my lessons learned, my daughters will know that I AM NOT PERFECT, nor do I expect them to be. My daughters will know that moms make mistakes and that I am always learning. Every time I do not show up the way I intended, I make sure they are aware that it is not their fault.

I believe what many of us are searching for is our mother's love. The challenge for mothers is to remember that your children want you to love them no matter what and without judgment. For the mothers struggling in your relationship with your daughter: meet them where they are, see them for who they are, and not who you want them to be. Listen without judgment, and look into their eyes with love. It's okay to share your feelings, really! Even if you know better, let your daughter think of a solution on her own. This will drive independence, confidence, and trust in them and in you. If you are always trying to fix her, she will always think something is wrong with her.

You may judge me for writing this next part and I am okay with that. When my mom passed, it was as if a huge weight lifted off my chest. Many of the pressures of being perfect, the guilt, and the people-pleasing started fading. I truly hate even writing that because I held onto those pressures and could have worked harder to let them go sooner. Now that those weights are lifted, I feel much closer to her, like she can really hear me now. I feel her presence everywhere. She is taking care of me in the most spiritually beautiful ways.

I have talked with her about writing this book, and she has been with me the entire journey. In fact, I feel her pride in me. Every time I had a moment of self-doubt, or needed to check in with her, a butterfly would find its way into my vision (either in-person or a picture would pop up). I even remember a time when I almost didn't complete this book and the fears had sunk in deep. My older daughter walked downstairs with a vibrant butterfly tee-shirt. *Okay,*

okay, snap out of it, Emily. You may not believe in signs, and that's okay, but it gave me the hope I needed to squash the doubts.

BREAKING THE CYCLE

I hope you are walking away with the feeling that you are not alone. I hope you feel supported and have more tools in your toolbox. And that you are valued and worth it!

At the age of 90, I asked my grandmother (who raised nine children and married a war vet) an important question.

"What's the one most essential piece of advice you could pass along?"

"One day at a time, that's really all you can do." I hear these words almost daily, especially when it feels like I am in the thick of another phase/growth spurt with my kids or season of my own personal growth. My grandpa turned 100 years old as I wrote this book. He told me, "to always look forward. The past already happened, there's nothing we can do. But we have a choice to move forward, and we have a choice as to what that looks like."

Pause + Reflect

- How do you want to show up?
- What energy do you want to bring?
- Are you ready to grow so big that even you have to get to know yourself again?
- What investments are you ready to make to show yourself that you are worthy, loved, and have a purpose?

Remember: You are enough. Guilt is a liar. Let go of toxicity. Your life is 100% your responsibility. You have a choice. Set boundaries. Take care of yourself. Be resistant to barriers. Show forgiveness and gratitude.

As Thomas Jefferson once said, "If you want something you've never had, you must be willing to do something you've never done."

EPILOGUE

After writing this book, with a deeper reflection, I realized I experienced yet another shift in perspective with more wisdom and understanding. It made me wonder, *what kind of child was I like for my mother? Did I cause her to be this way? I can't go back there, right?* I remember anytime we had a major blow out fight, I chose to only communicate with her through letters. This was the only way I felt heard. If I got it all out on paper, she would have my words to read without interruption or immediate defensive reaction.

Even though our relationship significantly improved towards the end of her time on earth, I still never really felt understood. As an adult, that continued to bother me. So it makes me wonder, was writing this book the ultimate healing I needed to break free, to feel heard completely and wholeheartedly?

Although I couldn't find the written letters, I did save the emails. Reading her words after she passed, brought on an entirely new realization. I saw them in a new light and read them with a new heart. It appeared that she really was trying to listen and build our relationships, but I couldn't hear that then. I saw her in a negative light and couldn't shake that from my story about her. These examples were from adulthood and warning you, she was known for *not* caring about grammar. She didn't have time for that.

2006

For context, I had been living in Arizona about a year and had difficulty with my first long-term relationship after she questioned what was wrong with us for not being married.

> *em you know i love you and would do anything in the world for you. and would stick up for you no matter what. we have had our differences in the past and i hope you can put them aside and let our love for each other matter most. i know that you can hurt the ones you love the most and i am truly sorry for all the things that i have done that hurt you. we do see things differently at times and sometimes that is good and natural. but i know that i love you and i know that you love me too!*
>
> *so after i hung up the phone and dad came into the room i was crying and he asked me what was wrong and i said i do not know why em is so upset with me --... i respect you i love you - so be patient and know i love you very much*
>
> *so can you please forgive me for the past and can our future be only good because i do love and respect you and i only want what is best for you and i want to be happy and and have good things happen for our relationship and mostly i want you to be happy!! i know i am rambling and i do miss being close to you I love you so very much!!! love mom xoxoxox*

2008

After I visited over Christmas vacation and she tried to control every aspect of my visit. I believe I was on anti-depressants/anti-anxiety medications and seeking counseling which she didn't see a purpose for, even made fun of my "happy pills."

> *Mom,*
>
> *I don't think you even know what you apologizing for. You say "we all make mistakes" and that is true. However, I don't say the things you say. I don't make fun of your choices. I don't mock your life decisions. I do, however, keep trying to help you. I am fighting for you. And, I feel that you are fighting against me. There is always someone*

for you to blame. It is always someone else's fault that you get worked up. I am really tired of always being picked apart. It makes me FEEL stupid, whether, you meant to or not. I am standing up for myself. That is what I have learned over the years, how to stand up for myself when I am feeling like someone is compromising me (even you). YOU NEED TO WORK ON SAYING WHAT YOU MEAN so that you don't permanently damage YOUR FAMILY.

I am DONE. I am done being treated like a child. I am done fighting for my mother who doesn't want my help. I am done believing that everything with you and I will be OK. Because, every time I start believing, I get disappointed. I feel like I have to be the adult with you. Again, I know I am not perfect and I have disappointed you as a daughter. I understand this and I should be better, do you understand that when I see my mother act like a child, its difficult for me to act normal. I already don't feel good enough for you or maybe that is just how you make me feel, I will decide that.

I want you to find happiness mom, I can see in you face how angry you are. Maybe life didn't turn out the way you planned. But, you only get one life and this is it. Make it better for yourself. I do believe in you, but you have to believe in yourself. You have to want it bad enough. FIND A WAY TO MAKE YOUR SELF HAPPIER! We do need you, and we do want you in our lives......I hope you believe me. I love you, Emily

2010

This email came after her solo visit when I was looking for my first home to buy. She was so upset with not being able to control whatever outcome that she barricaded my apartment door with her body and wouldn't let me leave. I had to trick her into "forgetting" something in my car and left to stay at a friend's.

i am sorry i did not listen to you and i was wrong for not listening to u i miss u so much and want to be there for you - i am so sorry em i miss you so much and love you love mom xoxoxox

141

My response to above:

*I absolutely loved sharing parts of my life with you and felt that you were really listening to me with an open heart. What I still don't like was mainly your **behavior** over my decisions and not respecting or listening to me. Then you used threatening words and child like behaviors to try to get your point across or try to get your way. THAT NEEDS TO STOP!!!!! I will not tolerate it or put up with it. I even cried to you and asked you to listen and you walked all over that making the situation about you.*

I understand that life can be stressful and challenging to each of us at different times and at the same time. We need to learn how to listen with patience and respect. You also need to learn how to channel these emotions so that they don't explode into rampages.

I do love you, very much. I am not mad at you, however, I am choosing not to openly discuss my issues with you right now. Your family does needs you, very much........hopefully you can see that with love.
- Emily

2011

After my brother's wedding, the same year one of her siblings passed away, she showed extreme erratic behavior.

It is of the utmost importance that our family gets back together (remembering the good old days). I want to be the mother i should be for you. I will continue to pray and I have found guidance as God is showing me the way. Pray for us ALL

Trust in our Love Trust in Me Trust in God Love MOM

2011

To my (extended) family...
I love you all dearly and you are a very important part of my life. I have been reading all of the emails that everyone is

142

sending. I wanted to let you know why I haven't been responding. I am exhausted with the issue of constantly discussing and trying to solve my mothers issues. I have been doing this for over 10 years and have sabotaged parts of myself in trying to fix her, save her, have a relationship with her, trust her, etc. I am finally focusing on myself and my life and don't want to feed anymore of my energy into things I can't control (and trust me .....I've tried!). She needs to find ways to help herself before she looses everyone that loves her.

I agree with being honest, straightforward, and real however being mean is never acceptable (even if SHE does it) and this will only aggravate her behavior. I'm not pointing fingers, however I look up to you and I don't want to loose that. At times, I already feel like I am loosing her and I am scared that it's getting worse.

I agree that we shouldn't tolerate her behavior because that only enables her and confuses her to the point that she thinks thats normal and acceptable behavior. I agree with calling her out and telling her how she makes us feel...she needs to know these things. One day it will matter to her.

I love you all and am grateful that we are in each others lives. Please pray for my father and his strength during this time.

Finally, please pray that one day my mother will come back to me. I miss her.

Love Emily

2011

From my mom to me:

i am making the best of each moment---trying to do things that are positive and that make me happy

-i want to be around positive people to get my energy from -i love helping people and doing good things

the past is the past and we can not change it-- the present is all we have as u stated---and so i will make each day the best i can!-

-i too agree that it is wasting my (little) quality time --
-with my own children which i treasure and that is why i do
not like sharing my time...

-i am acting more "appropriately" and will try (as i am
not perfect) to be better

- i love myself and who i am- and i love my family too i
am glad i have great friends-who i love and respect and
likewise-- it is a great feeling ! remember that we choose
each other !

-i am an adult—as are my children now---but they are
and always will be my children

-i am glad you love and believe in me and i hope that
you can respect and trust in me again soon !!

As I read through these old letters, a part of me started down the path of negative self-talk and doubt again. Memories, fights, and conversations arose. I reflected on moments where I remember being the worst version of myself. *Was I a total jerk to her? Did I cause her to be this way, to get worse over the years? Did I never see she was trying? No wonder she fought so hard. She really did love me but I could't see it.* So, I put her in this negative box and couldn't see her heart come through.

But here is the thing, I only knew what I knew with the skills that I had at that time. So, if I could go back to my younger self, what would I tell her now? I would tell her exactly what I am telling my older self today and the lessons I am teaching my own daughters.

Emily, your mother is teaching you very powerful insightful lessons that you will need to survive in this world. You will experience these lessons in every situation and within the depths of your soul. She is giving you exactly what you need to develop tools, protect your heart, and show up. You do not need to fight her. She is showing you exactly what you need to see in others. You need to experience this.

As a mother, I realize a little of what she may have been going through. *Could this be why I am so emotionally attached to the outcome with my children? Was she at her wits end?* Because some days I feel like I truly am. *Why do some days feel like such a struggle and what I am holding a tight grip on?* I read somewhere that your voice will become their inner voice. This totally scares me and at the same time, I am committed towards growth and a better relationship with my daughters.

If I ask my mother for help today, she says, with a heart full of love, "Emily, you are a great mom. You are doing the best you can. Do not ever doubt that. You are strong and kind and your girls are lucky to have you as their mom. You can do this, have faith in yourself."

I now believe that we are given what we need. That there was a reason for our struggle. It is there to see if we are going to let the struggle win or are we going to take the necessary measures to break free? It makes me wonder, could this be the reason why I feel like an imposter even publishing this book? Could this be why I am struggling so hard with my own daughters? Or is this my second chance – in a weird, twisted way?

After her death, I feel that my mother could finally hear me. But, I do not want to wait until I die for me to hear my daughters.

REFERENCES

Achor, S. (2018). The Happiness Advantage: How a Positive Brain Fuels Success in Work and Life. Currency, New York, NY.

Blondin, S. (2020). Heart Minded: How to Hold Yourself and Others in Love. Sounds True Inc., Boulder, CO.

Brody, L.S. (2017). The Fifth Trimester: The Working Mom's guide to Style, Sanity, and Big Success After Baby. Doubleday, New York.

Brown, B. (2017). Braving the Wilderness: the Quest for True Belonging and the Courage to Stand Alone. (2017). Random House Audio. New York, New York.

Byrne, R. (2016). The Secret. Atria Books; Beyond Words Pubs., New York, London.

Chapman, G. D. (2004). The 5 Love Languages: How to Express Heartfelt Commitment to your Mate. Northfield, Pub., Chicago.

Cloud, H. & Townsend, J.S. (2017). Boundaries: When to Say Yes, How to Say No to Take Control of Your Life. Zondervan, Grand Rapids, MI.

Dethmer, J. Chapman, D., & Klemp, K. (2015). The 15 Commitments of Conscious Leadership: A New Paradigm for Sustainable Success. Conscious Leadership Group.

Dorociak, K.E., Rupert, P.A., Bryant, F.B., & Zahniser, E. (2017). Development of a Self-Care Assessment for Psychologists. *Journal of Counseling Psychology, 64*(3), 325-334.

Dossey, B.M., Luck, S., & Schaub, B.G. (2014). Nurse Coaching: Integrative Approaches for Health and Wellbeing. International Nurse Coach Association, Miami, FL.

Doyle, G. (2020). Untamed. The Dial Press, New York, NY.

Frances, A. (2021). Rich as F*ck: More Money Than You Know What To Do With. Amanda Frances, Inc.

Gordon, S. (2021). Why using guilt trips is an ineffective parenting strategy. www.verywellfamily.com

Hendricks, G. (2009). The Big Leap. Conquer Your Hidden Fear and Take Life to the Next Level. HarperCollins, New York, NY.

Hollis, R. (2018). Girl Wash Your Face: Stop Believing the Lies About Who You Are so You Can Become Who You Were Meant to Be. Nelson Books. Nashville, TN.

Nagoski, E. & Nagoski, A. (2020). Burnout: The Secret to Unlocking the Stress Cycle. Ballantine Books, New York, NY.

Northrup, K. (2020). Do Less: A Revolutionary Approach to Time and Energy Management for Ambitious Women. Hay House, Inc. Carlsbad, CA.

Rodsky, E. (2019). Fair Play: A Game-Changing Solution for When You Have Too Much to Do (and More Life to Live). G.P. Putnam's Sons, New York, NY.

Rodsky, E. (2021). Find Your Unicorn Space: Reclaim Your Creative Life in a Too-Busy World. G.P. Putnam's Sons, New York, NY.

Schaub, R. & Schaub, B.G. (1997). Healing Addictions: The Vulnerable Model of Recovery. Albany, NY. Delmar Publishers.

Schwartz, L. (2017). Powerhouse Woman: How to Get Out of Your Own Way, Fullfill Your Unique Purpose, and Life a Powerful Life. Peacock Proud Press.

Siegel, D. J. & Hartzell, M. (2014). Parenting From the Inside Out: How a Deeper Self-Understanding Can Help You Raise Children Who Thrive. Findlay World, LLC, Solon, Ohio.

Sinek, S. (2009). Start with Why: How Great Leaders Inspire Everyone to Take Action. London, England. Penguin Books Ltd

Singer, M. (2007). The Untethered Soul: The Journey Beyond Yourself. New Harbinger Publications. Oakland, CA.

Wood, E. (2022). Matrescence: 4th Trimester Planning and Support. www.4thtrimesterplan.com/workshop

LESSON 1 NOTES

LESSON 2 NOTES

LESSON 3 NOTES

LESSON 4 NOTES

LESSON 5 NOTES

LESSON 6 NOTES

LESSON 7 NOTES

LESSON 8 NOTES

LESSON 9 NOTES

LESSON 10 NOTES

ACKNOWLEDGMENTS

We are not meant to do life or motherhood alone. I may have written the words, but this book would not be alive if it weren't for the many stories and life experiences along with the countless amount of energy and help that I received along the way.

So first and foremost, I want to thank my mother and grandmother who were raised during different times and had different challenges to deal with. As a mother, you loved the best way you knew how with the knowledge and experience you were given. Working to break old patterns was not against you but to adapt to the ever-changing world in order to enhance my survival and help my daughters thrive in our relationship.

To my father for letting me know that my voice matters. Thank you for spending countless hours caring for my children. I owe an enormous debt of pure gratitude to your calmness and generosity. You gave me permission to use this book as a form of healing. You told me that she approves and has hope that I feel the love that she tried to give me. I could feel that during my entire writing journey, and it couldn't be truer still today.

To my husband whose love makes me brave and confident. For believing that my work matters and that I better finally "do something with it." Your discipline and commitment to moving forward has strengthened me to my core. Your unwavering instinct really is "always right." Here's to never settling on anything less than extraordinary together.

To my brothers who always had my back, especially when I decided to write this vulnerable book. Growing up, you give me strength and built me back up with I was down. You gave me love when she didn't know how. You found ways to fill up my heart when it felt empty. Please know this love runs deep in my heart.

To my mother and father in-law for your unhesitating support and love throughout our journey together. From day one, you believed in me. You accepted me with open arms as if I was your daughter. When I felt compromised, you poured in more love. I hope you can feel how much I love and appreciate you.

To my BFF. We knew this would be a long-term relationship back in grade school. But, we had no idea the vital and challenging lessons we would learn from each other. You are my family by choice. I hope you never doubt that I have and will always love you.

To my own girl gang tribe. Thank you for picking me up when I'm down, showing up for me, and allowing me to be vulnerable, even if it's uncomfortable. Thank you for putting up with my stories for many years and even trying to help me through some of the worst of it. Thank you for your smiles, hugs, and positive messages. You know who you are and I love you all dearly! I would not be here today without the strength of these relationships. I hope I continue to attract amazing women who support each other and lift each other up. We are not meant to do this alone.

Thank you to all of the women whose stories inspired me to write this book. To the women I coach, I am deeply moved by your growth and willingness to heal and move forward. You have truly inspired me to continue to grow. You showed me how necessary this book is for other daughters to start their healing journey. The thoughts sat on a shelf for many years and during a major transitional time in my life, I decided to also take this leap of faith in completing it. Thank you for allowing me into your lives and trusting my guidance.

Thank you to my accountability partners. Lindsey Schwartz, CEO and founder of Powerhouse Women, for creating the space for female entrepreneurs to thrive together as a community and introducing me to Lauren Eckhardt, CEO of Burning Soul Collective. Both of you have pushed me beyond what I thought was possible and I am entirely grateful for your mentorships. It's not surprising why I picked your companies and gentle hands to hold me through this wild ride. Thank you to Allison Buehner, the most brilliant and eloquent editor. I appreciate your gentle patience with this first-time author. And of course, Denise Ervin, my original Nurse Coach, who provided space for me to discover my true passions and taught me the importance of pause and reflection.

To my daughters who really are my greatest teachers. Elaina, thank you for being my fire, my passion, my drive. Your determination, resilience, and strength are a force to be reckoned with. Watch out world! Allison, thank you for being the light in my heart after my mother died. Thank you for holding me (inside my belly) during that time. Your nurturing soul has been a constant comfort in my life. Writing this book has enhanced the necessary healing in my heart so that I can show up as the mother I really want to be for you both. If you don't hear my words, or feel my caring energy, please use this as my love letter to you.

Finally, I want to thank my readers and all the women out there who are daughters. It's because of you that I wrote this book. You are not alone.

ABOUT THE AUTHOR

EMILY S. JACOBS
DNP, RN, APRN, CCNS, NC-BC

Emily Jacobs is an author, speaker, board certified doctorate-prepared integrative nurse wellness coach, healthcare consultant, and thought leader.

With over 20 years of healthcare in nursing and corporate leadership experience, Emily started her endeavor consulting for companies and coaching individuals in health and wellness, building resiliency, adjusting to transitions, up-leveling leadership, burnout recovery, work/life balance, self-care strategies, setting healthy boundaries, and living a life they love.

Emily is a highly requested presenter and keynote speaker. She also became faculty of the Integrative Nurse Coach Academy training the future nurse coaches of the world.

What she learned the most from her private practice was that self-doubt and fear prevent us from believing in ourselves that we are worthy of creating an amazing life. Emily created a company to provide a safe space for others to overcome their biggest fears, move past self-doubt, and elevate their dreams because passion and perseverance is available for everyone.

Emily helps guide others through balance, boundaries, and recognizing toxicity. She challenges you to say goodbye to that stuck version of yourself in order to recognize that you are enough, you are loved, and **you have control of your choices.** She offers you the strength and clarity needed to knock down your barriers, heal your heart and find your way forward.

Emily Jacobs resides in Beverly Hills, Michigan with her husband and two vibrant daughters.

CONNECT WITH EMILY
Website: www.dremilyjacobs.com
Email: Emily@dremilyjacobs.com
Instagram: @dremilyjacobs

Lightning Source UK Ltd.
Milton Keynes UK
UKHW022103030123
414791UK00020B/302